LIVING LITURGY™

for Extraordinary Ministers of Holy Communion

Year C • 2022

Stephanie DePrez
Verna Holyhead, SGS
Orin E. Johnson
John T. Kyler

with
M. Roger Holland, II
and Ferdinand Okorie, CMF

LITURGICAL PRESS
Collegeville, Minnesota

www.litpress.org

ISSN 1933-3129

ISBN 978-0-8146-6604-3   ISBN 978-0-8146-6629-6 (ebook)

Presented to

_____

*in grateful appreciation
for ministering as an
Extraordinary Minister
of
Holy Communion*

_____

_____

(date)

USING THIS RESOURCE

Extraordinary typically refers to outstanding or exceptional. But extraordinary ministers of Holy Communion are "extra"ordinary in the sense of "in addition to" the ordinary (as well as being outstanding and exceptional!). Ordinary ministers of Holy Communion are the ordained and those properly installed as acolytes, usually seminarians. In parishes today there are simply not enough "ordinary" ministers of Holy Communion, so we call forth additional ministers, referred to as "extraordinary." Imagine how long the distribution of Communion would take if only the ordained or seminarians were those who distributed! It is not only because of need, however, that we have extraordinary ministers of Holy Communion. It is also by virtue of one's baptism. We parishioners are grateful that so many baptized Christians respond to the call to serve as extraordinary ministers of Holy Communion. In so doing we are reminded that we are all holy, and we are all called to ministry by virtue of our Christian baptism.

Preparing for This Ministry

Though different dioceses and parishes have slightly different preparation requirements for those who would be extraordinary ministers of Holy Communion, there is preparation nonetheless. We hope that this book will be a source of reflection for such preparation, and also for ongoing reflection throughout one's ministry. We know that it is not enough to simply attend a training event and never look back. Each ministry of the church requires regular prayer, reflection, reading, and thoughtfulness. This book is intended to assist with that process by providing prayers and reflection for each Sunday and for certain solemnities. This resource can also be used by groups who would like to share their faith with questions that prompt discussion.

Holy Communion for the Homebound and Sick

In the New Testament Letter of James we learn about the concern and care that the early Christians had for those members of their community who were sick. Such care and concern was a hallmark of Jesus's own ministry, and it has been a Christian charism ever since. Each week there are parishioners who are not able to join us for the liturgy, and so the Eucharist is brought to them as a sign of our unity. Extraordinary ministers of Holy Communion are often those who perform this ministry, and, in so doing, they extend the parish's reach to so many more fellow parishioners. This book is intended to be a resource for them as well.

Adapting This Resource for
Holy Communion for the Homebound and Sick

The Communion rite (Ordinary Rite of Communion of the Sick) is provided as a separate publication to this book and enclosed within. Those who are extraordinary ministers of Holy Communion have undoubtedly been made familiar with this rite as part of their preparation. This book may be adapted for use with the rite, by sharing the gospel reflection, the prayers, or even the reflection question, so that the visit becomes a true ministry. It is to be remembered that ministers are not mere functionaries. As such, extraordinary ministers of Holy Communion bring not only the presence of Christ in the eucharistic species, but the presence of Christ in their very person by virtue of their baptism. So this book has been designed with that in mind, and it can be used to assist with making this a meaningful encounter and ministry.

In today's gospel Jesus tells us to be mindful about the ways our hearts may grow drowsy. Let us remain awake and aware, asking for God's mercy and forgiveness . . .

Prayer

God of heaven and earth,
your ways are beyond our thinking,
your holiness is your gift to us.
To you, O Lord, I lift my soul.
Receive it, and bring me to completeness in you,
who are God, for ever and ever.
Amen.

Gospel   **Luke 21:25-28, 34-36**

Jesus said to his disciples: "There will be signs in the sun, the moon, and the stars, and on earth nations will be in dismay, perplexed by the roaring of the sea and the waves. People will die of fright in anticipation of what is coming upon the world, for the powers of the heavens will be shaken. And then they will see the Son of Man coming in a cloud with power and great glory. But when these signs begin to happen, stand erect and raise your heads because your redemption is at hand.

"Beware that your hearts do not become drowsy from carousing and drunkenness and the anxieties of daily life, and that day catch you by surprise like a trap. For that day will assault everyone who lives on the face of the earth. Be vigilant at all times and pray that you have the strength to escape the tribulations that are imminent and to stand before the Son of Man."

Brief Silence

For Reflection

Advent challenges us to let our hopes reach beyond cozy domesticity to the huge and human hope of a new creation. Just as a woman watches for the signs that the birth of her child is imminent, so Jesus urges his disciples to be alert to the birth pangs of the reign of God in all its fullness. In our present time, in the womb of human and cosmic history, God is nurturing and preparing for the birth of the new heaven and new earth. In the midst of any personal suffering, international tension, opportunist politics, or natural disasters that we might experience during these Advent weeks, the Word of God urges us to be people of hope. Nor are Christians to be the captives of frantic seasonal consumerism. We are called, rather, to be a people awake and alert to the promises of God already revealed, grateful for what has been liberating for us as Jesus's disciples in the year just past, and confident in the gifts of God that are yet to come.

✦ How do you live as a person of hope?

Brief Silence

Prayer

Loving God, thank you for the gift of this day and the opportunity to grow in relationship with you. May we bear witness to the hope you promise so that our hearts might be ready to receive you, as we remain faithful to your Gospel and the way of life to which we are called. **Amen**.

In today's gospel John cries out, "Prepare the way of the Lord." For the times our lives have not heralded God's coming, we ask for forgiveness and peace . . .

Prayer

Powerful and mighty Redeemer,
You have *done great things for us;*
we are filled with joy in your presence.
Help us always to remember the gladness of your salvation.
Give to us peace and perseverance always.
Through Christ our Lord.
Amen.

Gospel   Luke 3:1-6

In the fifteenth year of the reign of Tiberius Caesar, when Pontius Pilate was governor of Judea, and Herod was tetrarch of Galilee, and his brother Philip tetrarch of the region of Ituraea and Trachonitis, and Lysanias was tetrarch of Abilene, during the high priesthood of Annas and Caiaphas, the word of God came to John the son of Zechariah in the desert. John went throughout the whole region of the Jordan, proclaiming a baptism of repentance for the forgiveness of sins, as it is written in the book of the words of the prophet Isaiah: / *A voice of one crying out in the desert: / "Prepare the way of the Lord, / make straight his paths. / Every valley shall be filled / and every mountain and hill shall be made low. / The winding roads shall be made straight, / and the rough ways made smooth, / and all flesh shall see the salvation of God."*

Brief Silence

For Reflection

We are used to heavy earth-moving equipment and technology that builds roads to speed travelers on their way—cutting out sharp bends, smoothing treacherous bumps, straightening dangerous curves to give us a clearer and safer view of what is ahead or oncoming. Advent is the season of Christian "road work," with John the Baptist as our overseer. With John's voice, the church asks us both personally and communally to level and straighten out whatever is an obstacle or danger on our journey to God. What are the "potholes" in our discipleship, those sins of omission? From what do we need to be converted if we are to make the way smoother for others who find it difficult to travel to God because of our intolerant or erratic behavior? Do we indulge in outbursts of destructive "road rage" towards our sisters and brothers as we all try to follow the way of the gospel? Have we a kingdom vision that can enable us to see around the twists and turns of personal tragedy or ecclesial failure and recognize there an advent of Christ—his presence with us in the suffering, dying, and rising from these painful realities?

✦ Which paths in your own life might God be inviting you to straighten?

Brief Silence

Prayer

Loving God, thank you for the gift of this day and the opportunity to grow in relationship with you. May we heed the forerunner's voice and redirect our thoughts and actions to you alone, ever smoothing the rough edges of our heart so that we might remain faithful to your Gospel and the way of life to which we are called. **Amen**.

Today's gospel reminds us of Mary's great trust in God. For the times we have not been who we are called to be, we ask for mercy and forgiveness . . .

Prayer

God of every breath,
you put on our lips *a new song*
and inspire us to make a joyful noise to the glory of your name.
You have *done marvelous deeds* for us,
and your gift of music is wonderful indeed.
We thank and praise you, today and always.
Amen.

Gospel   Luke 1:26-38

The angel Gabriel was sent from God to a town of Galilee called Nazareth, to a virgin betrothed to a man named Joseph, of the house of David, and the virgin's name was Mary. And coming to her, he said, "Hail, full of grace! The Lord is with you." But she was greatly troubled at what was said and pondered what sort of greeting this might be. Then the angel said to her, "Do not be afraid, Mary, for you have found favor with God. Behold, you will conceive in your womb and bear a son, and you shall name him Jesus. He will be great and will be called Son of the Most High, and the Lord God will give him the throne of David his father, and he will rule over the house of Jacob forever, and of his Kingdom there will be no end." But Mary said to the angel, "How can this be, since I have no relations with a man?" And the angel said to her in reply, "The Holy Spirit will come upon you, and the power of the Most High will overshadow you. Therefore the child to be born will be called holy, the Son of God. And behold, Elizabeth, your relative, has also conceived a son in her old age, and this is the sixth month for her who was called barren; for nothing will be impossible for God." Mary said, "Behold, I am the handmaid of the Lord. May it be done to me according to your word." Then the angel departed from her.

Brief Silence

For Reflection

Today, we honor the Immaculate Conception of the Blessed Virgin Mary. Her role in God's saving plan for humanity is made vivid by the angelic salutation: Greetings! You have found favor with the Lord. The Blessed Mother hears in the angelic salutation the favorable action of God in her life that began at her conception, continues into the present moment, and now has become vivid in her self-consciousness. God's gift of divine favor to the Blessed Mother is the moving force in her life. Even though she is unaware of the profundity of God's grace in her life, it has guided and brought her to an expression of total self-professed cooperation with God's saving plan for humanity: "I am the handmaid of the Lord" and let God's will be done in me.

With the Blessed Mother's *fiat*, her role in God's plan for the salvation of the world is established. In this way, this maiden embraces her divine role that is far beyond personal ambition. Indeed, she gives up self-interest and chooses to work with God for the salvation of the world.

✦ Like Mary, each of us is chosen by God. How do you respond to God's call in your daily actions and interactions?

Brief Silence

Prayer

Loving God, thank you for the gift of this day and the opportunity to grow in relationship with you. May we follow the example of Mary's *fiat* and respond to your call with courage, generosity of spirit, and a willingness to give of ourselves for others so that we might remain faithful to your Gospel and the way of life to which we are called. **Amen**.

As we begin today's celebration, let us take a moment to ask for God's pardon and peace . . .

Prayer

God of the lowly,
you choose the weak and powerless
to elevate to strength and might.
Mary is our model in this,
and to her, in reverence, we proclaim:
you are the highest honor of our race.
Help us to recognize you
in the most marginalized among us.
Amen.

Gospel   Luke 1:26-38

The angel Gabriel was sent from God to a town of Galilee called Nazareth, to a virgin betrothed to a man named Joseph, of the house of David, and the virgin's name was Mary. And coming to her, he said, "Hail, full of grace! The Lord is with you." But she was greatly troubled at what was said and pondered what sort of greeting this might be. Then the angel said to her, "Do not be afraid, Mary, for you have found favor with God. Behold, you will conceive in your womb and bear a son, and you shall name him Jesus. He will be great and will be called Son of the Most High, and the Lord God will give him the throne of David his father, and he will rule over the house of Jacob forever, and of his Kingdom there will be no end." But Mary said to the angel, "How can this be, since I have no relations with a man?" And the angel said to her in reply, "The Holy Spirit will come upon you, and the power of the Most High will overshadow you. Therefore the child to be born will be called holy, the Son of God. And behold, Elizabeth, your relative, has also conceived a son in her old age, and this is the sixth month for her who was called barren; for nothing will be impossible for God." Mary said, "Behold, I am the handmaid of the Lord. May it be done to me according to your word." Then the angel departed from her.

Brief Silence

For Reflection

The Blessed Virgin Mary arrives to the Aztecs as one of their own to proclaim the good news of God's loving presence to the people, who are colonized and marginalized by Spanish conquistadors. Appearing to Juan Diego, speaking to him in his native language, the Blessed Mother identifies herself as his mother in a famous statement linked to the Blessed Mother: "Am I not here, I who am your Mother?"

After the gospel reading, the Blessed Mother arrives at the home of Elizabeth and Zechariah (Luke 1:40), bringing joy to Elizabeth and her child. Similarly, her presence to the Aztecs as Our Lady of Guadalupe brings hope and joy. When our church gathered at the Second Vatican Council, the Blessed Mother was recognized as a "model in faith and charity" (*Lumen Gentium* 53). She is venerated as a symbol of national unity and she is a Mother who unites God's children in the Americas and beyond. By her exemplary life of faith in God and charity toward God's children, the Blessed Mother teaches us that our faith in God should match our disposition to do good deeds toward one another.

✦ How do you show God's loving presence to the people you encounter who are excluded, exploited and hurting?

Brief Silence

Prayer

Loving God, thank you for the gift of this day and the opportunity to grow in relationship with you. You are intimately present to your people, especially those who suffer and carry heavy burdens. Give us the courage to speak against injustices everywhere so that we might remain faithful to your Gospel and the way of life to which we are called. **Amen**.

---

* Sunday, December 12, 2021, is the Third Sunday of Advent, and the Feast of Our Lady of Guadalupe is omitted this year. Our Lady of Guadalupe may be appropriately honored in the Homily, Universal Prayer, and hymns during the Sunday liturgy. If pastoral advantage calls for it (cf. GIRM, no. 376), a Votive Mass of Our Lady of Guadalupe may be celebrated on a weekday before or after December 12, with the proper readings and prayers.

In today's letter from Paul to the Philippians, we hear that the peace of God will guard our hearts and minds in Jesus. With prayer and petition let us acknowledge the times we have sinned . . .

Prayer

Great and Holy One of Israel,
you who have achieved for us wonders
    beyond measure,
and inspire in us confidence and courage.
We *cry out with joy and gladness*
for you are among us always.
In praise and awe, we make this humble gift of praise.
Amen.

Gospel   Luke 3:10-18

The crowds asked John the Baptist, "What should we do?" He said to them in reply, "Whoever has two cloaks should share with the person who has none. And whoever has food should do likewise." Even tax collectors came to be baptized and they said to him, "Teacher, what should we do?" He answered them, "Stop collecting more than what is prescribed." Soldiers also asked him, "And what is it that we should do?" He told them, "Do not practice extortion, do not falsely accuse anyone, and be satisfied with your wages."

Now the people were filled with expectation, and all were asking in their hearts whether John might be the Christ. John answered them all, saying, "I am baptizing you with water, but one mightier than I is coming. I am not worthy to loosen the thongs of his sandals. He will baptize you with the Holy Spirit and fire. His winnowing fan is in his hand to clear his threshing floor and to gather the wheat into his barn, but the chaff he will burn with unquenchable fire." Exhorting them in many other ways, he preached good news to the people.

Brief Silence

For Reflection

In the gospel a shout is heard: urgent, loud, seeming at first to be discordant with the joy of the other readings. John the Baptist is with us again.

John comes to us this third week of Advent as the awakener of our sense of social justice, the one who points to the clutter of selfish concerns and materialism that can suffocate our practical love for our brothers and sisters in the stale air of indifference or greed. We are called to be concerned not only with the material clothing of the naked, but also with covering with love the naked vulnerability of someone in need. To feed the hungry is not only to be concerned with the soup kitchen, but also to nourish one another with our compassionate concern. How can we, individually, or in our families, parishes, or other communities, respond today to John the Baptist? How can we plan ways in which we can give Christmas back to the ones to whom it really belongs: to the homeless, the refugees, the elderly, the sick, the hopeless young people, those with disabilities, all of whom are so often discarded like our cast-off Christmas wrappings?

✦ What do you think John the Baptist's answer would be if you asked him, "What should I do?"

Brief Silence

Prayer

Loving God, thank you for the gift of this day and the opportunity to grow in relationship with you. You remind us that we do not live as individuals. Help us to live in authentic community with all people, and empower us to care for all of our sisters and brothers so that we might remain faithful to your Gospel and the way of life to which we are called. **Amen**.

Today's gospel is about the importance of relationships. For the times we have not lived in right relationship with ourselves, others, and God, we ask for forgiveness . . .

Prayer

Lord,
you are our peace, hope, and salvation,
but at times we fail to recognize our need for you.
Make us turn to you;
help us daily choose conversion and your way.
Let us see your face and we shall be saved.
You are God, for ever and ever.
Amen.

Gospel   **Luke 1:39-45**

Mary set out and traveled to the hill country in haste to a town of Judah, where she entered the house of Zechariah and greeted Elizabeth. When Elizabeth heard Mary's greeting, the infant leaped in her womb, and Elizabeth, filled with the Holy Spirit, cried out in a loud voice and said, "Blessed are you among women, and blessed is the fruit of your womb. And how does this happen to me, that the mother of my Lord should come to me? For at the moment the sound of your greeting reached my ears, the infant in my womb leaped for joy. Blessed are you who believed that what was spoken to you by the Lord would be fulfilled."

Brief Silence

For Reflection

The Advent mystery tells us clearly that God has a special love for apparently unimportant people and places: for backwater Nazareth and its young woman; for the unnamed village of an old country priest and his aging wife; for the town of Bethlehem-Ephrathah which, by the time of the prophet Micah whom we heard in the first reading, had been eclipsed by Jerusalem in importance, despite the fact that the former was David's birthplace. The word of the Lord that came to Micah announces that a new future awaits this town for, like a woman in labor, its pain (of neglect) will be changed when it brings forth a future king who will fulfill the dreams as yet unrealized by the Davidic lineage. He will be shepherd of his flock, bringing peace and security. In such unimportant places and in unexpected ways, the Son of David will be born as this fulfillment of the dreams of his people. In us, too, such dreams will be fulfilled if we offer Jesus hospitality. God has given us the most wonderful of Christmas gifts: his own Son, wrapped in our human flesh.

✦ When was the last time you were so filled with joy and delight that you cried out loudly, like Elizabeth?

Brief Silence

Prayer

Loving God, thank you for the gift of this day and the opportunity to grow in relationship with you. Mary believed that what you spoke would be fulfilled. Open our own ears and our hearts to your unfurled promises so that we, like Mary, might remain faithful to your Gospel and the way of life to which we are called. **Amen**.

Today we rejoice at the birth of Jesus Christ, our Emmanuel. As we prepare to celebrate the mystery of the incarnation, we ask for pardon and peace for the times we have not lived as God incarnate . . .

Prayer

Christ the Lord,
you are *our Savior!*
We greet you today with a song,
ancient and ever-new.
You are salvation, you are glory,
you are justice, you are constancy.
Let us welcome you into our hearts,
and make for you a home there, now and always.
Amen.

Gospel   Luke 2:1-14 (Mass at Midnight)

In those days a decree went out from Caesar Augustus that the whole world should be enrolled. This was the first enrollment, when Quirinius was governor of Syria. So all went to be enrolled, each to his own town. And Joseph too went up from Galilee from the town of Nazareth to Judea, to the city of David that is called Bethlehem, because he was of the house and family of David, to be enrolled with Mary, his betrothed, who was with child. While they were there, the time came for her to have her child, and she gave birth to her firstborn son. She wrapped him in swaddling clothes and laid him in a manger, because there was no room for them in the inn.

Now there were shepherds in that region living in the fields and keeping the night watch over their flock. The angel of the Lord appeared to them and the glory of the Lord shone around them, and they were struck with great fear. The angel said to them, "Do not be afraid; for behold, I proclaim to you good news of great joy that will be for all the people. For today in the city of

David a savior has been born for you who is Christ and Lord. And this will be a sign for you: you will find an infant wrapped in swaddling clothes and lying in a manger." And suddenly there was a multitude of the heavenly host with the angel, praising God and saying: / "Glory to God in the highest / and on earth peace to those on whom his favor rests."

Brief Silence

For Reflection

Jesus was not born in the familiarity of his own home, not surrounded by celebrating family and friends. Mary's birth pangs and Joseph's shared pain come as they are on a journey and among strangers. The traditional interpretation of "no room for them in the inn" has been one of negative refusal to help an obviously pregnant, near-to-full-term woman and her husband, something that would be abhorrent to Middle Eastern hospitality. Could it be that Luke is already emphasizing that it is the poor who are willing to give what they have, even if this is only the humble hospitality of a room shared with the animals and a feeding-trough bed for the newborn rather than more conventional guest accommodation? Given that he is writing fifty or so years after the resurrection of Jesus, Luke has surely experienced this, been moved by it, and challenges his more affluent communities with it. How often, to our shame, have the poor witnessed this to us in our own times? We find the Child laid "today" not only in the feeding place of the eucharistic table but also in our sisters and brothers.

✦ The incarnation is an act of God's self-gift. How do you share yourself with others?

Brief Silence

Prayer

Loving God, thank you for the gift of this day and the opportunity to grow in relationship with you. Today we rejoice in you and celebrate your self-gift to us. Through the solidarity and hope of your incarnation may we remain faithful to your Gospel and the way of life to which we are called. **Amen**.

Today we celebrate the Holy Family, the relationship between Jesus, Mary, and Joseph. For the times we have failed to live in communion with others as one human family, we ask for pardon and peace . . .

Prayer

Embracing God,
you are always ready to welcome us home
into your loving arms.
Blessed are they who dwell in your house,
who live in your presence, and you in them.
Help us to know you, and be one with you, always.
Amen.

Gospel   Luke 2:41-52

Each year Jesus' parents went to Jerusalem for the feast of Passover, and when he was twelve years old, they went up according to festival custom. After they had completed its days, as they were returning, the boy Jesus remained behind in Jerusalem, but his parents did not know it. Thinking that he was in the caravan, they journeyed for a day and looked for him among their relatives and acquaintances, but not finding him, they returned to Jerusalem to look for him. After three days they found him in the temple, sitting in the midst of the teachers, listening to them and asking them questions, and all who heard him were astounded at his understanding and his answers. When his parents saw him, they were astonished, and his mother said to him, "Son, why have you done this to us? Your father and I have been looking for you with great anxiety." And he said to them, "Why were you looking for me? Did you not know that I must be in my Father's house?" But they did not understand what he said to them. He went down with them and came to Nazareth, and was obedient to them; and his mother kept all these things in her heart. And Jesus advanced in wisdom and age and favor before God and man.

Brief Silence

For Reflection

For Mary and Joseph, as for all parents, there is the pain of allowing their child his independence, his identity, loving him, not possessing him or punishing him, but not fully understanding him. Surely a sword passes also through Joseph's heart when, in response to Mary's words about "your father and I," and as if gently contradicting her, Jesus refers to "my Father." For us, as for Joseph, commitment to gospel priorities will always cause some pain. Parents know this in a special and poignant way. For now, this "passover" of the adolescent Jesus is a theological sign of what is to come.

After this, Jesus returns to Nazareth with Mary and Joseph and is obedient to them, and Luke concludes his narrative of Jesus's childhood by telling us that "Jesus advanced in wisdom and age and favor before God and man." An aspect of doing his Father's will was his openness to being graced by the precious relationships of his family at Nazareth. Children and parents in every age and culture are meant to be grace for one another.

✦ Family relationships are not always easy. How does today's celebration invite you to examine your own familial relationships?

Brief Silence

Prayer

Loving God, thank you for the gift of this day and the opportunity to grow in relationship with you. Just as Mary and Joseph find you in the temple, let us avail ourselves to you, trusting your presence as we remain faithful to your Gospel and the way of life to which we are called. **Amen**.

As we begin this new calendar year and celebrate this great solemnity of Mary, the Holy Mother of God, we pause and pray, mindful of our own sinfulness and need for God's mercy . . .

Prayer

Gracious One,
you who are justice and *mercy*,
bless us and be with us;
let your face shine upon us.
Show us your ways,
with your mother as guide and companion.
May Mary be mother to us,
and another gift of your presence.
Amen.

Gospel   **Luke 2:16-21**

The shepherds went in haste to Bethlehem and found Mary and Joseph, and the infant lying in the manger. When they saw this, they made known the message that had been told them about this child. All who heard it were amazed by what had been told them by the shepherds. And Mary kept all these things, reflecting on them in her heart. Then the shepherds returned, glorifying and praising God for all they had heard and seen, just as it had been told to them.

When eight days were completed for his circumcision, he was named Jesus, the name given him by the angel before he was conceived in the womb.

Brief Silence

For Reflection

Having been visited by angels, the shepherds risk a hasty journey down from the hills to the town. And when they return to their flocks, to their ordinary life, they return as people of praise, giving glory on their small piece of earth to what the angels had glorified in the vast heavens above them.

Mary hears what the shepherds repeat to her and, in contrast to their rush and excitement, around her there is silence. For a second time, she is "reflecting on" what she has heard. The Greek word that Luke uses is from *symballo*, with the meaning of "throwing together," "discussing." Mary tries to "throw things together": her own human experience, the divine power which she knows is working in her, the vulnerable child of her womb, and what the shepherds have told her—the holy, messianic naming of the Son. She is surely the model for our pondering of the Word, for the times of reflective silence that we all need to find, for the challenge that disciples of Jesus accept: to constantly try to treasure the good news about Jesus, and treasure this in spite of the often contradictory voices we hear.

✦ How do you, like Mary, leave room in your heart to contemplate God and God's incredible works?

Brief Silence

Prayer

Loving God, thank you for the gift of this day and the opportunity to grow in relationship with you. Upon hearing the message of the angels, the shepherds move in haste to share the glory of God. Help us to share your glory with the people we encounter as we remain faithful to your Gospel and the way of life to which we are called. **Amen.**

Today's feast of the Epiphany celebrates the arrival and homage of the magi. We, too, give Jesus homage by our lives. For the times we have not lived according to our call, we ask God for forgiveness and peace . . .

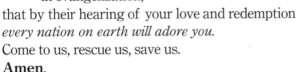

Prayer

King of Glory,
you are the God of all peoples.
Inspire in us courage and perseverance
    in evangelization,
that by their hearing of your love and redemption
every nation on earth will adore you.
Come to us, rescue us, save us.
Amen.

Gospel   Matt 2:1-12

When Jesus was born in Bethlehem of Judea, in the days of King Herod, behold, magi from the east arrived in Jerusalem, saying, "Where is the newborn king of the Jews? We saw his star at its rising and have come to do him homage." When King Herod heard this, he was greatly troubled, and all Jerusalem with him. Assembling all the chief priests and the scribes of the people, he inquired of them where the Christ was to be born. They said to him, "In Bethlehem of Judea, for thus it has been written through the prophet: / *And you, Bethlehem, land of Judah, / are by no means least among the rulers of Judah; / since from you shall come a ruler, / who is to shepherd my people Israel."* / Then Herod called the magi secretly and ascertained from them the time of the star's appearance. He sent them to Bethlehem and said, "Go and search diligently for the child. When you have found him, bring me word, that I too may go and do him homage." After their audience with the king they set out. And behold, the star that they had seen at its rising preceded them, until it came and stopped over the place where the child was. They were overjoyed at seeing the star, and on entering the house they saw the child with Mary his mother. They prostrated themselves and did him homage. Then they opened their treasures and offered him gifts of gold, frankincense, and myrrh. And having been warned in a dream not to return to Herod, they departed for their country by another way.

Brief Silence

For Reflection

In the Gentile Magi, the divisions of culture, religions, and nation are reconciled because, as we respond with the antiphon to Psalm 72, "Lord, every nation on earth will adore you." A multicultural society and church are witnesses to the inclusiveness that Christ asks of us.

The most important gift we can offer Christ, the gift richer than any gold, frankincense, or myrrh is, of course, the wealth of our love and the fragrant readiness of suffering which this will inevitably entail. In the gifts that the wise ones offer to the Christ child there is again the hint of the paschal mystery: the myrrh of embalming, the frankincense that fragranced the temple sacrifices and burned before the Holy of Holies, the gold of precious value. The Magi go home by another route when they realize that they are being manipulated by hypocrisy and jealous power-seeking. It is, Matthew suggests, often the strangers and outsiders—and today read the asylum seekers or the unpretentious poor or those who work for justice—who reveal to us, as individuals and as nations, how and what we should be seeking and how to come home to this truth.

✦ How do you witness to the inclusion that Christ offers?

Brief Silence

Prayer

Loving God, thank you for the gift of this day and the opportunity to grow in relationship with you. When the magi saw the star at its rising, they searched diligently for the Christ child to offer gifts and praise. Guide us, too, as we search for your presence in our world, as we remain faithful to your Gospel and the way of life to which we are called. **Amen**.

In baptism you claim us for yourself. As we are sprinkled with these waters, let us prepare ourselves to enter this celebration . . .

Prayer

Glorious God,
you are dressed in a mantle of light
and dwell in a palace of wisdom and truth.
You too are humility, service, and love,
freely given to your people in covenant with you.
O bless the Lord, my soul.
Amen.

Gospel   Luke 3:15-16, 21-22

The people were filled with expectation, and all were asking in their hearts whether John might be the Christ. John answered them all, saying, "I am baptizing you with water, but one mightier than I is coming. I am not worthy to loosen the thongs of his sandals. He will baptize you with the Holy Spirit and fire."

After all the people had been baptized and Jesus also had been baptized and was praying, heaven was opened and the Holy Spirit descended upon him in bodily form like a dove. And a voice came from heaven, "You are my beloved Son; with you I am well pleased."

Brief Silence

For Reflection

In his account of the baptism of Jesus, Luke includes an insight on the significance of prayer. Several times in his gospel Luke sets important events in Jesus's life and mission in the context of prayer (e.g., Luke 6:12-13; 9:28; 22:42-46). Jesus dies with the words of Psalm 31:5 on his lips. The baptism of the Lord could be called a prayer event, for Luke does not describe the moment of baptism but rather its aftermath. It is Jesus's prayer that tears open the heavens for the descent of the Holy Spirit and the revelation of his true identity by the Father's voice that acclaims him as the Beloved Son on whom God's favor rests.

It is the same for us. Prayer is a necessary part of our identity as baptized sons and daughters of God. It opens heaven to us and reveals who we are—for, in a very real sense, we are who we pray. At prayer we struggle to hear what God is calling us to be, to know who we are in our deepest truth, at the still point where the Spirit has descended into our depths and anointed us for mission.

✦ What does it mean for you to live as God's beloved?

Brief Silence

Prayer

Loving God, thank you for the gift of this day and the opportunity to grow in relationship with you. In baptism you choose us for yourself, and claim us as your own. Empower us to live the radical reality of our baptism, that we remain faithful to your Gospel and the way of life to which we are called. **Amen**.

In today's gospel we hear the story of the wedding at Cana in Galilee where Jesus's disciples first began to know him. For the times we have failed to prioritize our relationship with you, we ask for forgiveness and healing . . .

Prayer

Wondrous God,
you are so far beyond our
    understanding,
but so approachable,
yearning for us to know and love you.
Help us to share your *marvelous deeds to all the nations,*
for by doing so, we better know you
and bring all together in your holiness and truth.
Amen.

Gospel   John 2:1-11

There was a wedding at Cana in Galilee, and the mother of Jesus was there. Jesus and his disciples were also invited to the wedding. When the wine ran short, the mother of Jesus said to him, "They have no wine." And Jesus said to her, "Woman, how does your concern affect me? My hour has not yet come." His mother said to the servers, "Do whatever he tells you." Now there were six stone water jars there for Jewish ceremonial washings, each holding twenty to thirty gallons. Jesus told them, "Fill the jars with water." So they filled them to the brim. Then he told them, "Draw some out now and take it to the headwaiter." So they took it. And when the headwaiter tasted the water that had become wine, without knowing where it came from—although the servers who had drawn the water knew—, the headwaiter called the bridegroom and said to him, "Everyone serves good wine first, and then when people have drunk freely, an inferior one; but you have kept the good wine until now." Jesus did this as the beginning of his signs at Cana in Galilee and so revealed his glory, and his disciples began to believe in him.

Brief Silence

For Reflection

At the wedding in Cana, the bridegroom is a shadowy, silent, and inactive presence, a foil for the next time a bridegroom is mentioned in John 3:29, when John the Baptist acclaims Jesus to be the Bridegroom of his people and himself as the best man who, according to cultural practice, presents the Bridegroom to the bride Israel, and then withdraws.

The purificatory jars at Cana numbered six, a symbolic number of incompleteness. At Jesus's "hour" there will be a seventh jar, when from the clay of his passion-fired humanity there will flow the wine of his blood, not only for purification but for exultant transformation.

The wine-become-blood redeems and purifies his bride, the church. It allows her to participate in the Lord's own death and nourishes her with the life of the Resurrection. Accordingly, the wine of "the wedding of the Lamb" is the mystical image for the entire paschal feast of the Lord, the feast of the new and eternal covenant. It is this mystery of word and wine, this paschal celebration, which we celebrate at every Sunday Eucharist. We are now the wedding guests waiting to be filled with the sacramental wine.

✦ Jesus reveals an important part of himself at the wedding feast of Cana. How does Jesus reveal himself to you?

Brief Silence

Prayer

Loving God, thank you for the gift of this day and the opportunity to grow in relationship with you. At the wedding feast at Cana you revealed yourself to all present at the celebration. Reveal yourself to us that we remain faithful to your Gospel and the way of life to which we are called. **Amen.**

In today's letter from Paul to the Corinthians we hear that we are all part of Christ's body. For the times we have not fully lived this calling, we ask our loving God for pardon and peace . . .

Prayer

Eternal Logos,
your words are Spirit and life.
Your laws are perfect and trustworthy,
leading us to the fullness of your presence.
Give us open ears to hear you, you who still speak today,
often through the poor and marginalized among us.
Amen.

Gospel   Luke 1:1-4; 4:14-21

Since many have undertaken to compile a narrative of the events that have been fulfilled among us, just as those who were eye-witnesses from the beginning and ministers of the word have handed them down to us, I too have decided, after investigating everything accurately anew, to write it down in an orderly sequence for you, most excellent Theophilus, so that you may realize the certainty of the teachings you have received.

Jesus returned to Galilee in the power of the Spirit, and news of him spread throughout the whole region. He taught in their synagogues and was praised by all.

He came to Nazareth, where he had grown up, and went according to his custom into the synagogue on the sabbath day. He stood up to read and was handed a scroll of the prophet Isaiah. He unrolled the scroll and found the passage where it was written:
/ The Spirit of the Lord is upon me, / because he has anointed me / to bring glad tidings to the poor. / He has sent me to proclaim

liberty to captives / and recovery of sight to the blind, / to let the oppressed go free, / and to proclaim a year acceptable to the Lord. / Rolling up the scroll, he handed it back to the attendant and sat down, and the eyes of all in the synagogue looked intently at him. He said to them, "Today this Scripture passage is fulfilled in your hearing."

Brief Silence

For Reflection

As we begin to journey with Luke through the semi-continuous gospel readings of Year C, it is appropriate that the first four verses are read to remind us of Luke's purpose in writing his two-part good news, the gospel and Acts of the Apostles. In the latter, it is the church that is committed to doing in the power of the Spirit of Jesus what he himself did in the days of his flesh. Theophilus, who is addressed in verse 3, was probably a significant Christian and a patron of Luke. "God-lover" though he may be, there is always more truth to be discovered, a greater commitment to be made, a new excitement about the tradition that has been handed down by those who were both eyewitnesses and servants of the word. Luke is not one of these, but he is respectful of what he has received from them. Using his own human gifts and guided by the Holy Spirit, he is eager to record, order, and interpret the Jesus tradition for the sake of his patron and the wider community of believers. "Today" we are among those believers, gathered into the Liturgy of the Word, into the presence of Christ.

✦ How do you respond when you learn something new or surprising about someone you have known for a long time?

Brief Silence

Prayer

Loving God, thank you for the gift of this day and the opportunity to grow in relationship with you. As you did for those gathered in the temple, surprise us with the presence that we might truly know you as we remain faithful to your Gospel and the way of life to which we are called. **Amen**.

In today's gospel, Jesus is rejected for being prophetic. For the times we have ignored or shunned prophetic voices we encounter, we ask for God's pardon and peace . . .

Prayer

Merciful God,
those who know you may never be
    shamed,
those who love you know your hope and justice.
Help me to be one with you,
to *sing of your salvation* in the midst of all peoples,
you who are my stronghold and safety.
Amen.

Gospel   Luke 4:21-30

Jesus began speaking in the synagogue, saying: "Today this Scripture passage is fulfilled in your hearing." And all spoke highly of him and were amazed at the gracious words that came from his mouth. They also asked, "Isn't this the son of Joseph?" He said to them, "Surely you will quote me this proverb, 'Physician, cure yourself,' and say, 'Do here in your native place the things that we heard were done in Capernaum.'" And he said, "Amen, I say to you, no prophet is accepted in his own native place. Indeed, I tell you, there were many widows in Israel in the days of Elijah when the sky was closed for three and a half years and a severe famine spread over the entire land. It was to none of these that Elijah was sent, but only to a widow in Zarephath in the land of Sidon. Again, there were many lepers in Israel during the time of Elisha the prophet; yet not one of them was cleansed, but only Naaman the Syrian." When the people in the synagogue heard this, they were all filled with fury. They rose up, drove him out of the town, and led him to the brow of the hill on which their town had been built, to hurl him down headlong. But Jesus passed through the midst of them and went away.

Brief Silence

For Reflection

The animosity that Jesus will encounter throughout his life, the opposition that will lead him to martyrdom, seems to be concentrated into this event as the Lukan sign of what is to come. Jesus dares to confront the synagogue assembly with the memory of God's grace shown to those beyond the community of Israel by referring to two other prophets: Elijah and Elisha. For the poor widow of Zarephath, a Gentile, Elijah miraculously replenished her meager store of oil and grain during a famine (1 Kgs 17:8-16); when commanded by Elisha to wash in the waters of the Jordan, the Syrian leper, Naaman, was healed (2 Kgs 5:9-14).

When Jesus tries to make the people face the truth and consequences of their own Scriptures—and his ministry—this unwelcome reproach to their consciences enrages them. They choose, as religious communities may so often do, to have a selective memory about their tradition. On this occasion, the crowd drives Jesus to a hill from which they can either throw him down or stone him. But Jesus passes through their midst and "went away." He goes on to another hill, another angry crowd, to be thrown down onto a cross and lifted high. If today's Christian communities are closed or divided, Jesus will pass again through their midst and walk away.

✦ Who are some of the prophetic voices calling out in the world today?

Brief Silence

Prayer

Loving God, thank you for the gift of this day and the opportunity to grow in relationship with you. There are times when it seems like our voices go unheard and our example ignored. Be with us as we strive to be prophetic, remaining faithful to your Gospel and the way of life to which we are called. **Amen**.

In today's gospel Peter exclaims, "Depart from me, Lord, for I am a sinful man." Like Peter, we at times recognize our own sinfulness and dependence on God's love, pardon, and peace . . .

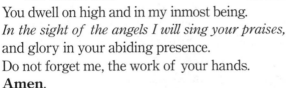

Prayer
O God,
you are kindness and truth, and hear
me when I call.
You dwell on high and in my inmost being.
In the sight of the angels I will sing your praises,
and glory in your abiding presence.
Do not forget me, the work of your hands.
Amen.

Gospel   Luke 5:1-11

While the crowd was pressing in on Jesus and listening to the word of God, he was standing by the Lake of Gennesaret.
He saw two boats there alongside the lake; the fishermen had disembarked and were washing their nets. Getting into one of the boats, the one belonging to Simon, he asked him to put out a short distance from the shore. Then he sat down and taught the crowds from the boat. After he had finished speaking, he said to Simon, "Put out into deep water and lower your nets for a catch." Simon said in reply, "Master, we have worked hard all night and have caught nothing, but at your command I will lower the nets."
When they had done this, they caught a great number of fish and their nets were tearing. They signaled to their partners in the other boat to come to help them. They came and filled both boats so that the boats were in danger of sinking. When Simon Peter saw this, he fell at the knees of Jesus and said, "Depart from me, Lord, for I am a sinful man." For astonishment at the catch of fish

they had made seized him and all those with him, and likewise James and John, the sons of Zebedee, who were partners of Simon. Jesus said to Simon, "Do not be afraid; from now on you will be catching men." When they brought their boats to the shore, they left everything and followed him.

Brief Silence

For Reflection

We may admire Peter's humble profession of his unworthiness to associate with Jesus. But could there not also be a fear of the deep waters that Peter might be letting himself into, waters that would be less troubled if Jesus just went away? Are there times when we have said to God, "Why me?" when being asked to cope with this commitment, this vocation, this suffering?

One day a young woman whose daughter had just given birth to a child with Down Syndrome, asked her mother in tears, "Why me?" Her mother replied, "Why? Because of all my children, you are the one whom I would choose—and God has chosen—to be the mother of this child who needs so much love."

At the dawn of the Third Millennium, John Paul II reminded the church of this passage of Luke's gospel: *Duc in altum!* Put out into the deep! These words ring out for us today. They invite us to remember the past with gratitude, to live the present with enthusiasm, and to look forward to the future with confidence. More than two decades later, how are we measuring up to this challenge?

✦ How might you be more attentive to the voice of God's invitation in your own life?

Brief Silence

Prayer

Loving God, thank you for the gift of this day and the opportunity to grow in relationship with you. As you filled the nets to bursting, fill our heats with your exceptional love. Through our daily labor may we remain faithful to your Gospel and the way of life to which we are called. **Amen**.

Today we hear the prophet Jeremiah proclaim, "Blessed is the one who trusts in the LORD, whose hope is in the LORD." For the times we have not trusted in God and instead placed our hope in things not of God, we ask for forgiveness and healing . . .

Prayer

Watchful God,
you guide us in your ways,
your laws are the delight of those who follow you.
Blessed are they who hope in you,
who meditate on you and your life-giving presence.
Draw us ever closer to you and your providence.
Amen.

Gospel   **Luke 6:17, 20-26**

Jesus came down with the Twelve and stood on a stretch of level ground with a great crowd of his disciples and a large number of the people from all Judea and Jerusalem and the coastal region of Tyre and Sidon. And raising his eyes toward his disciples he said: / "Blessed are you who are poor, / for the kingdom of God is yours. / Blessed are you who are now hungry, / for you will be satisfied. / Blessed are you who are now weeping, / for you will laugh. / Blessed are you when people hate you, and when they exclude and insult you, and denounce your name as evil on account of the Son of Man. Rejoice and leap for joy on that day! Behold, your reward will be great in heaven. For their ancestors treated the prophets in the same way. / But woe to you who are rich, / for you have received your consolation. / Woe to you who are filled now, /

for you will be hungry. / Woe to you who laugh now, / for you will grieve and weep. / Woe to you when all speak well of you, / for their ancestors treated the false prophets in this way."

Brief Silence

For Reflection

For Luke, the poor were not just the poor in spirit (as in Matt 5:3); they were the economically impoverished, the people on the margins, pushed there by a society that did not take seriously the covenant responsibility to which Moses and the prophets had called them. The poor are specially loved by God, not so much because of what they are, but because of what God is—the compassionate defender of the weak and powerless. As the theologian Gustavo Gutierrez wrote: "God has a preferential love for the poor not because they are necessarily better than others, morally or religiously, but because they are living in an inhuman situation that is contrary to God's will. The ultimate basis for the privileged position of the poor is not in the poor themselves but in God, in the graciousness and universality of God's agapeic love" ("Song and Deliverance," in R. S. Sugirtharajah, ed., *Voices from the Margin*).

As individuals, church, governments, our justice re-presents God's justice to the world. The poor, hungry, weeping, and persecuted people are those for whom the church calls us to make a special option, one with both personal and political consequences.

✦ What are some of the personal and political consequences of your relationship with Christ?

Brief Silence

Prayer

Loving God, thank you for the gift of this day and the opportunity to grow in relationship with you. Your way of life issues a great reversal where the poor abound with plenty and the hungry eat their fill. Let us rejoice in your ways, not our own, as we remain faithful to your Gospel and the way of life to which we are called. **Amen**.

In today's gospel, Jesus gives us an overview of the Christian moral life. For the times we have done wrong and for the times we have failed to do good, we ask for God's pardon, healing, and peace . . .

Prayer

Forgiving God,
those who live in your love
know your compassion and kindness.
You are *kind and merciful* to all,
and your generosity is plentiful;
in wonder and awe we stand in your presence.
Your holy people thank you, you who are our one God.
Amen.

Gospel   Luke 6:27-38

Jesus said to his disciples: "To you who hear I say, love your enemies, do good to those who hate you, bless those who curse you, pray for those who mistreat you. To the person who strikes you on one cheek, offer the other one as well, and from the person who takes your cloak, do not withhold even your tunic. Give to everyone who asks of you, and from the one who takes what is yours do not demand it back. Do to others as you would have them do to you. For if you love those who love you, what credit is that to you? Even sinners love those who love them. And if you do good to those who do good to you, what credit is that to you? Even sinners do the same. If you lend money to those from whom you expect repayment, what credit is that to you? Even sinners lend to sinners, and get back the same amount. But rather, love your enemies and do good to them, and lend expecting nothing back; then your reward will be great and you will be children of the Most High, for he himself is kind to the ungrateful and the wicked. Be merciful, just as your Father is merciful.

"Stop judging and you will not be judged. Stop condemning and you will not be condemned. Forgive and you will be forgiven. Give, and gifts will be given to you; a good measure, packed together, shaken down, and overflowing, will be poured into your lap. For the measure with which you measure will in return be measured out to you."

Brief Silence

For Reflection

Shortly after the 1989 murder in San Salvador of the six Jesuits and their housekeeper and her daughter, the theologian Jon Sobrino, SJ, spoke at a Salvadoran refuge in London about the tragedy. Around the altar at the refuge were cards with the names of deceased family members and friends of those who lived there. As they were not allowed to go to the cemetery to put flowers on the graves, they had painted flowers around the names. One card with no flowers read: "Our dead enemies." At the conclusion of the Eucharist, an old man explained to Jon: "As we are Christians, you know, we believe that our enemies should be on the altar, too. They are our brothers, in spite of the fact that they kill and murder us."

To love our enemies is surely hard, unreasonable, yet it is also the most radical obedience that Jesus asks of his disciples as he continues his Sermon on the Plain. To love our enemies who victimize us makes us no longer victims; we become free people whose behavior is determined by no one else—except the Christ of whom we are disciples.

✦ What does it mean for you to "Be merciful, just as your Father is merciful?"

Brief Silence

Prayer

Loving God, thank you for the gift of this day and the opportunity to grow in relationship with you. When you challenge us to forgive sinners and love our enemies, you challenge is to grow in your own image and likeness. May we share mercy abundantly as we remain faithful to your Gospel and the way of life to which we are called. **Amen**.

In today's gospel Jesus reminds us that every tree is known by its own fruit. For the times we have not borne fruit, or borne fruit that is rotten, we ask God for pardon and peace . . .

Prayer

Omnipotent God,
you yearn to be known by all peoples in all lands,
and command each of us to
go out to all the world and tell the good news.
May our feet never tire,
and our evangelization always be clear and strong.
In your name we pray.
Amen.

Gospel   **Luke 6:39-45**

Jesus told his disciples a parable, "Can a blind person guide a blind person? Will not both fall into a pit? No disciple is superior to the teacher; but when fully trained, every disciple will be like his teacher. Why do you notice the splinter in your brother's eye, but do not perceive the wooden beam in your own? How can you say to your brother, 'Brother, let me remove that splinter in your eye,' when you do not even notice the wooden beam in your own eye? You hypocrite! Remove the wooden beam from your eye first; then you will see clearly to remove the splinter in your brother's eye.

"A good tree does not bear rotten fruit, nor does a rotten tree bear good fruit. For every tree is known by its own fruit. For people do not pick figs from thornbushes, nor do they gather grapes from brambles. A good person out of the store of goodness in his heart produces good, but an evil person out of a store of evil produces evil; for from the fullness of the heart the mouth speaks."

Brief Silence

For Reflection

The mass media and politicians are a source of many words in contemporary society. The "doublespeak" we get can be dishonest and dangerous. We need the wisdom and discernment of which Jesus speaks in today's gospel reading. Recent history has many examples of "doublespeak" that may be so familiar to our ears that our hearts no longer have a Christian reaction. "The final solution" meant the genocide of six million Jews; "collateral damage" in war means the killing of innocent civilians; a prison's "management unit" is a solitary confinement block. We need to take the pulse of our newspapers, TV, and governments to make a Christian diagnosis of such language and its reporters.

Our words can be used to praise and thank God for his love, as we do in today's responsorial psalm. Worshipping in the house of the Lord and planted in God's fidelity, the faithful person is like a fertile palm, or as enduring in their love of God as a great Lebanon cedar. Designated as a "Sabbath song," this psalm is an appropriate response for us as we gather as a Sunday community of faith and worship in God's house and as a temple of living stones.

✦ Which "splinters" in someone else's eyes do you find yourself preoccupied with and how can you turn that focus on yourself, someone you can actually change?

Brief Silence

Prayer

Loving God, thank you for the gift of this day and the opportunity to grow in relationship with you. So often we remain focused on the shortcomings of others—our family members, coworkers, and friends. Instead, help us to deeply examine the areas where we need growth, that we might produce good as we remain faithful to your Gospel and the way of life to which we are called. **Amen.**

As we begin this holy season of Lent, a time of prayer, fasting, and almsgiving, we take a moment to recall our sins and ask for God's forgiveness . . .

Prayer

God of Goodness,
you bring life and renewal to all
    creation,
and mercy to the repentant.
Be merciful, O Lord, for we have sinned.
Pride, waste, envy, and apathy abound;
you are greater than these.
As we return to you, help us know your love and compassion.
Amen.

Gospel   Matt 6:1-6, 16-18

Jesus said to his disciples: "Take care not to perform righteous deeds in order that people may see them; otherwise, you will have no recompense from your heavenly Father. When you give alms, do not blow a trumpet before you, as the hypocrites do in the synagogues and in the streets to win the praise of others. Amen, I say to you, they have received their reward. But when you give alms, do not let your left hand know what your right is doing, so that your almsgiving may be secret. And your Father who sees in secret will repay you.

"When you pray, do not be like the hypocrites, who love to stand and pray in the synagogues and on street corners so that others may see them. Amen, I say to you, they have received their reward. But when you pray, go to your inner room, close the door, and pray to your Father in secret. And your Father who sees in secret will repay you.

"When you fast, do not look gloomy like the hypocrites. They neglect their appearance, so that they may appear to others to be fasting. Amen, I say to you, they have received their reward. But when you fast, anoint your head and wash your face, so that you may not appear to be fasting, except to your Father who is hidden. And your Father who sees what is hidden will repay you."

Brief Silence

For Reflection

We are fond of logos. Schools, businesses, sporting clubs and teams, community groups, travel agencies, all use them to say—often superficially: "You belong to us, and we belong to each other." As we prepare to enter into the Season of Lent, the church presents us with a "logo." Not a very elegantly designed logo, this cruciform smudge of ash on our foreheads, but then neither was the crucifixion of Jesus elegant. Nor is the cross of ash gentle and fragrant like the first cross that was traced on us with the oils of catechumens and chrism at baptism. Our first liturgical fingerprinting recorded our identity as "Christian," as one committed to living and dying and rising with Christ. The cross another brother or sister fingers on us today is rougher, grittier, dirtier than the cross of baptismal oils—because that it how our lives have become. As we receive the ashes, the words of both options are stark and urgent: "Repent, and believe in the Gospel" or "Remember that you are dust, and to dust you shall return." Remember what Lent is all about.

✦ How do you hope to draw closer to the Lord during this Lenten season as you prepare to renew your baptismal promises at Easter?

Brief Silence

Prayer

Loving God, thank you for the gift of this day and the opportunity to grow in relationship with you. As we begin this holy season of Lent may we recommit ourselves to prayer, fasting and almsgiving, that we might more fully know your Easter joy as we remain faithful to your Gospel and the way of life to which we are called. **Amen**.

Today's gospel reminds us of the importance of prioritizing God in our lives, even over comfort and riches. For the times we have not made God a priority, we ask for forgiveness . . .

Prayer

Divine Compassion,
you who are holy and wholeness,
we turn to you with contrite hearts, saying:
Be with me, Lord, when I am in trouble.
Wash us, cleanse us, make us new in you.
Help us to trust in your love and mercy.
Amen.

Gospel   Luke 4:1-13

Filled with the Holy Spirit, Jesus returned from the Jordan and was led by the Spirit into the desert for forty days, to be tempted by the devil. He ate nothing during those days, and when they were over he was hungry. The devil said to him, "If you are the Son of God, command this stone to become bread." Jesus answered him, "It is written, *One does not live on bread alone.*" Then he took him up and showed him all the kingdoms of the world in a single instant. The devil said to him, "I shall give to you all this power and glory; for it has been handed over to me, and I may give it to whomever I wish. All this will be yours, if you worship me." Jesus said to him in reply, "It is written: / *You shall worship the Lord, your God, / and him alone shall you serve.*" / Then he led him to Jerusalem, made him stand on the parapet of the temple, and said to him, "If you are the Son of God, throw yourself down from here, for it is written: / *He will command his angels concerning you, to guard you,* / and: / *With their hands they will support you,* / *lest you dash your foot against a stone."* / Jesus said to him in reply, "It also says, *You shall not put the Lord, your God, to the test."* When the devil had finished every temptation, he departed from him for a time.

Brief Silence

For Reflection

The people of first century Palestine, living under the oppression of the Roman Empire, were hoping for political redemption. If Jesus seizes power and glory, suggests the devil, what he could do for them! But Jesus knows what this would mean: power and authority handed to him by the tempter would bring with it oppression and violence (Luke 4:1-14). Instead, Jesus will go the more sacrificial way of service rather than domination. He will wait to receive the kingdom from his Father rather than from the ruler of a "counter-kingdom." Jesus will establish a healing reign over sick bodies, tormented psyches, and a troubled cosmos. We are only too familiar with scenarios of unjust wars and political compromise in the lust for power. We certainly need to take a stand against these, but perhaps we are less conscious of the compromises in ourselves: bargaining for a little more status and authority at the expense of others. We can often be tempted to serve personal success rather than fidelity to God, our own reputation rather than the needs of our brothers and sisters. "God alone shall you serve" will involve Christians in the self-sacrificing obedience of Jesus.

✦ How do you respond to the temptations that you encounter each day?

Brief Silence

Prayer

Loving God, thank you for the gift of this day and the opportunity to grow in relationship with you. In you alone do we find the riches we seek and the joy for which we long. Be with us as we face temptation, that we may remain faithful to your Gospel and the way of life to which we are called. **Amen**.

In today's gospel we encounter the transfiguration of Jesus. Knowing our own need for transformation, we ask for God's healing and forgiveness for the times we have sinned . . .

Prayer

Luminous God,
you are our *light and salvation.*
Teach us not to be afraid,
and show us how to place our trust in you,
eternal and omnipotent, present and intimate God.
Encourage us to dwell securely in your loving arms.
Amen.

Gospel   Luke 9:28b-36

Jesus took Peter, John, and James and went up the mountain to pray. While he was praying his face changed in appearance and his clothing became dazzling white. And behold, two men were conversing with him, Moses and Elijah, who appeared in glory and spoke of his exodus that he was going to accomplish in Jerusalem. Peter and his companions had been overcome by sleep, but becoming fully awake, they saw his glory and the two men standing with him. As they were about to part from him, Peter said to Jesus, "Master, it is good that we are here; let us make three tents, one for you, one for Moses, and one for Elijah." But he did not know what he was saying. While he was still speaking, a cloud came and cast a shadow over them, and they became frightened when they entered the cloud. Then from the cloud came a voice that said, "This is my chosen Son; listen to him." After the voice had spoken, Jesus was found alone. They fell silent and did not at that time tell anyone what they had seen.

Brief Silence

For Reflection

With Moses on Mount Sinai, Daniel's Son of Man, and Mary of Nazareth, the overshadowing cloud was witness to and symbol of God's transfiguring presence. Now it embraces the tabernacle of Jesus's body and those who are his companions. Terrified, they enter and hear the Father's assurance, given only to Jesus at his baptism but now announced to disciples of all times: "This is my chosen Son; listen to him." Then there is silence, and Jesus alone is with them. They will go down from the mountain, onto the plain; and the struggle to understand Jesus goes on. On the plains of our everyday life, we struggle to respond to the Father's command: to listen to the Son, to become children of light in his light, brothers and sisters who are ready to risk the unfamiliar and new because we are enveloped in the security of God's presence and promise. After the mountain of Jesus's transfiguration comes the hill of his crucifixion. Our pilgrim legs have to be strong for both climbs, and though we may not always recognize it, the "mountaintop" experiences are often occasions where God allows us to catch our breath for the next and harder ascents.

✦ What are your own experiences of transformation? How is Christ calling you to transformation today?

Brief Silence

Prayer

Loving God, thank you for the gift of this day and the opportunity to grow in relationship with you. Transform our hearts, just as you transfigured on the mountain. May the radiant glory of your transfiguration help us remain faithful to your Gospel and the way of life to which we are called. **Amen**.

In today's reading from Exodus, Moses responds to God's call on the mountain in the burning bush. For the times we have remained indifferent to God's call in our own lives, we ask God for peace and healing . . .

Prayer

Most Holy Name,
our praise adds nothing to your greatness,
but our offering of praise is itself your gift to us.
You are *kind and merciful,*
just, gracious, and worthy of our worship.
Help us be always mindful of your holiness,
in reverence, wonder, and awe.
Amen.

Gospel   Luke 13:1-9

Some people told Jesus about the Galileans whose blood Pilate had mingled with the blood of their sacrifices. Jesus said to them in reply, "Do you think that because these Galileans suffered in this way they were greater sinners than all other Galileans? By no means! But I tell you, if you do not repent, you will all perish as they did! Or those eighteen people who were killed when the tower at Siloam fell on them—do you think they were more guilty than everyone else who lived in Jerusalem? By no means! But I tell you, if you do not repent, you will all perish as they did!"

And he told them this parable: "There once was a person who had a fig tree planted in his orchard, and when he came in search of fruit on it but found none, he said to the gardener, 'For three years now I have come in search of fruit on this fig tree but have found none. So cut it down. Why should it exhaust the soil?'

He said to him in reply, 'Sir, leave it for this year also, and I shall cultivate the ground around it and fertilize it; it may bear fruit in the future. If not you can cut it down.'"

Brief Silence

For Reflection

In today's gospel the crowd reminds Jesus of what happened to a group of Galileans who had been worshipping God when they themselves became sacrificial offerings at the hands of Pilate's henchman. Jesus recognizes the unspoken but implied question: *Big sinners, big suffering?* and answers with an explicit *No*. He himself raises the issue of eighteen people who were killed when a tower near the tower of Siloam accidentally collapsed on them for no known reason.

Neither of these incidents, says Jesus, is about God's punishment of the victims' sinfulness, although human nature is sometimes quick to make such a judgment. They show, rather, the fragility of our lives and the suddenness with which death can overwhelm us. We can be tempted to query, privately or publicly, the truth of our response to Psalm 103, "The Lord is kind and merciful," but the laws of nature are not to be equated with the laws of morality.

Jesus uses these events to make one point: what happened was sudden, with no time to avoid the catastrophes. But there is a much greater catastrophe on which the people need to focus: their unpreparedness for the merciful yet just judgment of God.

✦ Where have you seen a fruitless fig tree bloom in your life? What was your process for cultivating fruit?

Brief Silence

Prayer

Loving God, thank you for the gift of this day and the opportunity to grow in relationship with you. Do not give up on us, but give our hearts the opportunity to bloom and grow. In your generous love help us remain faithful to your Gospel and the way of life to which we are called. **Amen**.

In today's gospel, Jesus shares a parable to illustrate the immense love God has for us. For the times we have rejected that love, we ask God for forgiveness and mercy . . .

Prayer

Sustaining God,
you give us what we need in due season,
and support us through all adversities.
Let us *taste and see the goodness* that is you:
strength, courage, compassion,
moderation, prudence, wisdom,
zeal, fervor, and love.
We make this prayer through the One who feeds us,
Christ the Lord.
Amen.

Gospel   Luke 15:1-3, 11-32

Tax collectors and sinners were all drawing near to listen to Jesus, but the Pharisees and scribes began to complain, saying, "This man welcomes sinners and eats with them." So to them Jesus addressed this parable: "A man had two sons, and the younger son said to his father, 'Father give me the share of your estate that should come to me.' So the father divided the property between them. After a few days, the younger son collected all his belongings and set off to a distant country where he squandered his inheritance on a life of dissipation. When he had freely spent everything, a severe famine struck that country, and he found himself in dire need. So he hired himself out to one of the local citizens who sent him to his farm to tend the swine. And he longed to eat his fill of the pods on which the swine fed, but nobody gave him any. Coming to his senses he thought, 'How many of my father's hired workers have more than enough food to eat, but here am I, dying from hunger. I shall get up and go to my father and I shall say to him, "Father, I have sinned against heaven and against you. I no longer deserve to be called your son; treat me as you would treat one of your hired workers.'" So he got up and went back to his father. While he was still a long way off, his father caught sight of him, and was filled with compassion. He ran to his son, embraced him and kissed him. His son said to him, 'Father, I have sinned against heaven and against you; I no longer deserve to be called your son.' But his father ordered his servants, 'Quickly bring the finest robe and put it on him; put a ring on his finger and sandals on his feet. Take the fattened calf and slaughter it. Then let us celebrate with a feast, because this son of mine was dead, and has come to life again; he was lost, and has been found.' Then the celebration began. Now the older son had been out in the field and, on his way back, as he neared the house, he heard the sound of music and dancing. He called one of the servants and asked what this might mean. The servant said to him, 'Your brother has returned and your father has slaughtered the fattened calf because he has him back safe and sound.' He became angry, and when he refused to enter the house, his father came out and pleaded with him. He said to his father in reply, 'Look, all these years I served you and not once did I disobey your orders; yet you never gave me even a young goat to feast on with my friends. But when your son returns who swallowed up your property with prostitutes, for him you slaughter the fattened calf.' He said to him, 'My son, you are here with me always; everything I have is yours. But now we must celebrate and rejoice, because your brother was dead and has come to life again; he was lost and has been found.'"

Brief Silence

For Reflection

In the parable of the Prodigal Son, the loving father allows his younger son the freedom to reject his love. The boy's desires lead him where he certainly did not intend to go when he left home: to enslavement to a Gentile boss in a Gentile pigsty, to starvation, and to physical and spiritual impoverishment. By looking after pigs he makes himself ritually unclean, so squandering a second inheritance: his Jewish faith. At this crisis point, the boy "comes to his senses"—works it all out in the first person: *I* will do this and that; *I* will go home and do the work of a hired hand so that *I* can pay back my debts; *I* will explain everything to my father and express my regret at what *I* have done. But coming to his senses doesn't reconcile the son; coming to his father will.

During Lent, the church calls us to remember the gifts of God that we have squandered and pay attention to our spiritual "pigsty." With great wisdom, she also knows that we need this time of heightened awareness of our compassionate Father who embraces us in the outstretched arms of the Crucified.

✦ Which relationships might God be calling you to restore? How will you approach this process of healing and reconciliation?

Brief Silence

Prayer

Loving God, thank you for the gift of this day and the opportunity to grow in relationship with you. As the father embraces his son, we trust that you call us, even when we are still a long way off. Through the gift of reconciliation help us remain faithful to your Gospel and the way of life to which we are called. **Amen.**

In today's gospel an angry crowd stands ready to condemn and punish the woman caught in adultery. For the times we have condemned others and sought punishment instead of reconciliation, we ask for God's pardon and peace . . .

Prayer

Worker of Wonders,
you have *done great things for us; we are filled with joy.*
Your greatest act of love is your self-sacrifice,
your death which gives life, eternal and complete.
We can do nothing but receive your freely given gift,
and offer gratitude and praise.
Amen.

Gospel   John 8:1-11

Jesus went to the Mount of Olives. But early in the morning he arrived again in the temple area, and all the people started coming to him, and he sat down and taught them. Then the scribes and the Pharisees brought a woman who had been caught in adultery and made her stand in the middle. They said to him, "Teacher, this woman was caught in the very act of committing adultery. Now in the law, Moses commanded us to stone such women. So what do you say?" They said this to test him, so that they could have some charge to bring against him. Jesus bent down and began to write on the ground with his finger. But when they continued asking him, he straightened up and said to them, "Let the one among you who is without sin be the first to throw a stone at her." Again he bent down and wrote on the ground. And in response, they went away one by one, beginning with the elders. So he was left alone with the woman before him. Then Jesus straightened up and said to her, "Woman, where are they? Has no one condemned you?" She replied, "No one, sir." Then Jesus said, "Neither do I condemn you. Go, and from now on do not sin any more."

Brief Silence

For Reflection

As we pray the Scriptures reflectively, we can let our imagination lead us deeper into Jesus's heart, into his human memory and experience. Reflecting on this gospel, might we wonder if, on that temple morning, he remembered his own mother: the fear she must have experienced, the gossip she probably endured about her pregnancy. And did Jesus also remember the gentle and just Joseph, who would not cast a stone?

Far away from the temple, in our own experience, are we tempted to use the sins of others to mask our own self-righteousness and failures? What attitude do we show to those who claim the right to dispense death by war, capital punishment, euthanasia, abortion, or subtle defamation? Are we brave enough to oppose their ethic, in personal encounter or by the ballot box? Do we pray that they will change their hearts? And are some of us still most condemnatory about those who sin against the two commandments that seem to be written larger than the other eight in our Christian psyches, those concerned with things sexual? What we need to heap up in our own hearts and in our church is compassion that heals, not stones that hurt.

✦ When have you been the adulterous woman from today's gospel? When have you been the Pharisee?

Brief Silence

Prayer

Loving God, thank you for the gift of this day and the opportunity to grow in relationship with you. Just as you do not cast stones at us, may we refrain from casting stones at others. Remind us that your mercy is always greater than our sins as we strive to remain faithful to your Gospel and the way of life to which we are called. **Amen**.

As we celebrate Palm Sunday, our proclamations of joy and acclamation quickly turn to shouts of condemnation and death. For the times when our words and actions have been inconsistent with who we are called to be, we ask for God's mercy and forgiveness . . .

Prayer

My God,
your presence is mysterious and, at times, hard to perceive.
We cry *"my God, why have you abandoned me,"*
yet we know you are always near.
Help us to be mindful of your compassion,
your suffering with us, in all times and places.
Amen.

Gospel   Luke 23:1-49 (or Luke 22:14–23:56)

The elders of the people, chief priests and scribes, arose and brought Jesus before Pilate. They brought charges against him, saying, "We found this man misleading our people; he opposes the payment of taxes to Caesar and maintains that he is the Christ, a king." Pilate asked him, "Are you the king of the Jews?" He said to him in reply, "You say so." Pilate then addressed the chief priests and the crowds, "I find this man not guilty." But they were adamant and said, "He is inciting the people with his teaching throughout all Judea, from Galilee where he began even to here."

On hearing this Pilate asked if the man was a Galilean; and upon learning that he was under Herod's jurisdiction, he sent him to Herod who was in Jerusalem at that time. Herod was very glad to see Jesus; he had been wanting to see him for a long time, for he had heard about him and had been hoping to see him perform some sign. He questioned him at length, but he gave him no answer. The chief priests and scribes, meanwhile, stood by accusing him harshly. Herod and his soldiers treated him contemptuously and mocked him, and after clothing him in resplendent garb, he sent him back to Pilate. Herod and Pilate became friends that very day, even though they had been enemies formerly. Pilate then summoned the chief priests, the rulers, and the people and said to them, "You brought this man to me and accused him of inciting the people to revolt. I have conducted my investigation in your presence and have not found this man guilty of the charges you have brought against him, nor did Herod, for he sent him back to us. So no capital crime has been committed by him. Therefore I shall have him flogged and then release him."

But all together they shouted out, "Away with this man! Release Barabbas to us."—Now Barabbas had been imprisoned for a rebellion that had taken place in the city and for murder.— Again Pilate addressed them, still wishing to release Jesus, but they continued their shouting, "Crucify him! Crucify him!" Pilate addressed them a third time, "What evil has this man done? I found him guilty of no capital crime. Therefore I shall have him flogged and then release him." With loud shouts, however, they persisted in calling for his crucifixion, and their voices prevailed. The verdict of Pilate was that their demand should be granted. So he released the man who had been imprisoned for rebellion and murder, for whom they asked, and he handed Jesus over to them to deal with as they wished.

As they led him away they took hold of a certain Simon, a Cyrenian, who was coming in from the country; and after laying the cross on him, they made him carry it behind Jesus. A large crowd of people followed Jesus, including many women who mourned and lamented him. Jesus turned to them and said, "Daughters of Jerusalem, do not weep for me; weep instead for yourselves and for your children for indeed, the days are coming when people will say, 'Blessed are the barren, the wombs that never bore and the breasts that never nursed.' At that time people will say to the mountains, 'Fall upon us!' and to the hills,

'Cover us!' for if these things are done when the wood is green what will happen when it is dry?" Now two others, both criminals, were led away with him to be executed.

When they came to the place called the Skull, they crucified him and the criminals there, one on his right, the other on his left. Then Jesus said, "Father, forgive them, they know not what they do." They divided his garments by casting lots. The people stood by and watched; the rulers, meanwhile, sneered at him and said, "He saved others, let him save himself if he is the chosen one, the Christ of God." Even the soldiers jeered at him. As they approached to offer him wine they called out, "If you are King of the Jews, save yourself." Above him there was an inscription that read, "This is the King of the Jews."

Now one of the criminals hanging there reviled Jesus, saying, "Are you not the Christ? Save yourself and us." The other, however, rebuking him, said in reply, "Have you no fear of God, for you are subject to the same condemnation? And indeed, we have been condemned justly, for the sentence we received corresponds to our crimes, but this man has done nothing criminal." Then he said, "Jesus, remember me when you come into your kingdom." He replied to him, "Amen, I say to you, today you will be with me in Paradise."

It was now about noon and darkness came over the whole land until three in the afternoon because of an eclipse of the sun. Then the veil of the temple was torn down the middle. Jesus cried out in a loud voice, "Father, into your hands I commend my spirit"; and when he had said this he breathed his last.

Here all kneel and pause for a short time.

The centurion who witnessed what had happened glorified God and said, "This man was innocent beyond doubt." When all the people who had gathered for this spectacle saw what had happened, they returned home beating their breasts; but all his acquaintances stood at a distance, including the women who had followed him from Galilee and saw these events.

Brief Silence

For Reflection

Scourged and mocked, Jesus is led out to his death—the innocent, nonviolent victim of the sin of the world. Simon of Cyrene is made to help him carry his cross, but Jesus is the Servant who will still reach out to others. When some of the women of Jerusalem follow him like a mourning chorus, Jesus ministers to their grief. On Golgotha, Jesus ministers also to the poor criminal who recognizes him as a just one. Lover of sinners to the end, Jesus allows this thief to "steal" Paradise from him. Then quietly, Jesus escapes, like a bird freed from a trap, into his Father's hands.

For a moment, then, we go down silently on our knees, rising to hear the faith of a non-Gentile proclaim before the human wreck: "This man was innocent beyond doubt." This is the faith that will take us through Holy Week and through the killing fields in our own world. Hopefully, too, we will minister like Joseph of Arimathea: taking the wounded body of Christ, our suffering sisters and brothers, off their crosses, wrapping them in our compassion, and advocating for them before the powerful with gentle but brave persistence.

✦ How have you emptied yourself for others? How have others emptied themselves for you?

Brief Silence

Prayer

Loving God, thank you for the gift of this day and the opportunity to grow in relationship with you. You are self-gift, embodied in humility and vulnerability. Following your example may we give of ourselves for others as we strive to remain faithful to your Gospel and the way of life to which we are called. **Amen.**

As we begin this Sacred Triduum and commemorate your acts of humility and service, we call to mind the times we have not lived and loved in your example . . .

Prayer

God of the Heavenly Banquet,
you join with us as saving victim,
and nourish us with your very body
    and blood.
Our blessing-cup is a communion with you,
who are mystery and paradox,
and live and reign for ever and ever.
Amen.

Gospel   John 13:1-15

Before the feast of Passover, Jesus knew that his hour had come to pass from this world to the Father. He loved his own in the world and he loved them to the end. The devil had already induced Judas, son of Simon the Iscariot, to hand him over. So, during supper, fully aware that the Father had put everything into his power and that he had come from God and was returning to God, he rose from supper and took off his outer garments. He took a towel and tied it around his waist. Then he poured water into a basin and began to wash the disciples' feet and dry them with the towel around his waist. He came to Simon Peter, who said to him, "Master, are you going to wash my feet?" Jesus answered and said to him, "What I am doing, you do not understand now, but you will understand later." Peter said to him, "You will never wash my feet." Jesus answered him, "Unless I wash you, you will have no inheritance with me." Simon Peter said to him, "Master, then not only my feet, but my hands and head as well." Jesus said to him, "Whoever has bathed has no need except to have his feet washed, for he is clean all over; so you are clean, but not all." For he knew who would betray him; for this reason, he said, "Not all of you are clean."

So when he had washed their feet and put his garments back on and reclined at table again, he said to them, "Do you realize what I have done for you? You call me 'teacher' and 'master,' and rightly so, for indeed I am. If I, therefore, the master and teacher, have washed your feet, you ought to wash one another's feet. I have given you a model to follow, so that as I have done for you, you should also do."

Brief Silence

For Reflection

The fact that the people called Israel had once been strangers and slaves in Egypt, who were liberated by their God, was to have historical, religious, and ethical reverberations for the Jewish people down through the generations. They were to remember liturgically this Jewish Passover in every generation, a remembrance that pulls past, present, and future into a personal and communal "we" and a glorious but demanding "today."

Every Eucharist is a celebration of the Passover of the Lord, accomplished definitively in the blood of Christ, the Lamb of God, which marks us for salvation. As a nighttime community, we come together on this Holy Thursday to share the meal of salvation and commit ourselves once again to the journey into which Christ calls us: into freedom and away from the slavery of sin. With the words of Psalm 116 on our lips we toast the goodness of God, no longer as the psalmist does from a cup of sacrificial libation at the temple, but from the blessing cup of the sacramental blood of the risen Christ. We pledge ourselves publicly in the liturgical assembly to keep our promises to God.

✦ What does *humility* mean to you?

Brief Silence

Prayer

Loving God, thank you for the gift of this day and the opportunity to grow in relationship with you. In the gift of the Eucharist you remind us that life in you cannot be separated from service of others. May your example keep us attuned to the needs of all as we strive to remain faithful to your Gospel and the way of life to which we are called. **Amen**.

This is resurrection day! Alleluia! Knowing that we do not always walk in the light of the resurrection, we ask for God's healing presence in our lives . . .

Prayer

God of the Empty Tomb,
in seven days you made all creation;
on the eighth day you made all things new by rising from the
    dead.
This is the day the Lord has made; let us rejoice and be glad.
In newness of life we praise and exalt your name.
Amen.

Gospel   **John 20:1-9 (or Luke 24:1-12 or Luke 24:13-35)**

On the first day of the week, Mary of Magdala came to the tomb early in the morning, while it was still dark, and saw the stone removed from the tomb. So she ran and went to Simon Peter and to the other disciple whom Jesus loved, and told them, "They have taken the Lord from the tomb, and we don't know where they put him." So Peter and the other disciple went out and came to the tomb. They both ran, but the other disciple ran faster than Peter and arrived at the tomb first; he bent down and saw the burial cloths there, but did not go in. When Simon Peter arrived after him, he went into the tomb and saw the burial cloths there, and the cloth that had covered his head, not with the burial cloths but rolled up in a separate place. Then the other disciple also went in, the one who had arrived at the tomb first, and he saw and believed. For they did not yet understand the Scripture that he had to rise from the dead.

Brief Silence

For Reflection

How does one extract hope from tragedy? How is one able to move on from trauma and find the strength and courage to keep living? In John's account of the discovery of the empty tomb on what we have come to know as Easter morning, Mary Magdalene (Mary of Magdala), planning to prepare the body of Jesus for burial, discovers an empty tomb. Beyond simply shock and surprise, this experience was trauma on top of trauma.

Much like the crucifixion of Jesus, the lynching of Black men and women were public spectacles, a traumatic event for members of the Black community, especially for members of the victim's family. Lynchings in the United States, like crucifixions by the Roman Empire, were intended as a deterrent, a public warning and display of oppressive, institutional power.

Yet, it is in the midst of great tragedy that God's power is revealed. It is through God's grace that we are able to experience hope in the midst of tragedy and trauma. The resurrection of Jesus not only represents hope in the midst of tragedy but also the transformation of physical and spiritual death to life.

✦ When have you encountered the newness of life that springs from death?

Brief Silence

Prayer

Loving God, thank you for the gift of this day and the opportunity to grow in relationship with you. In your resurrection you remind us that death never wins. Life and love always prevail. Help us share this life and love with others as we strive to remain faithful to your Gospel and the way of life to which we are called. **Amen**.

In today's gospel Jesus shares the gift of peace with his disciples. May this water remind us of God's healing presence in our lives . . .

Prayer

Divine Mercy,
your son reigns over all with a merciful love,
born of compassion and humility.
To him we sing:
give thanks to the Lord for he is good,
his love is everlasting.
Help us who doubt to always trust in you,
who live and reign for ever and ever.
Amen.

Gospel   **John 20:19-31**

On the evening of that first day of the week, when the doors were locked, where the disciples were, for fear of the Jews, Jesus came and stood in their midst and said to them, "Peace be with you." When he had said this, he showed them his hands and his side. The disciples rejoiced when they saw the Lord. Jesus said to them again, "Peace be with you. As the Father has sent me, so I send you." And when he had said this, he breathed on them and said to them, "Receive the Holy Spirit. Whose sins you forgive are forgiven them, and whose sins you retain are retained."

Thomas, called Didymus, one of the Twelve, was not with them when Jesus came. So the other disciples said to him, "We have seen the Lord." But he said to them, "Unless I see the mark of the nails in his hands and put my finger into the nailmarks and put my hand into his side, I will not believe."

Now a week later his disciples were again inside and Thomas was with them. Jesus came, although the doors were locked, and stood in their midst and said, "Peace be with you." Then he said to Thomas, "Put your finger here and see my hands, and bring your hand and put it into my side, and do not be unbelieving, but believe." Thomas answered and said to him, "My Lord and my God!" Jesus said to him, "Have you come to believe because you have seen me? Blessed are those who have not seen and have believed."

Now Jesus did many other signs in the presence of his disciples that are not written in this book. But these are written that you may come to believe that Jesus is the Christ, the Son of God, and that through this belief you may have life in his name.

Brief Silence

For Reflection

Nowhere in the gospels is Thomas ever described as "doubting." He has been outspoken, generous, ready to go to death with his master (John 11:16). At the Last Supper he is honest enough to say aloud what the other disciples were most likely thinking: that none of them *are* sure where Jesus is heading. But like his companions who did not accept the testimony of Mary Magdalene about Jesus's resurrection, Thomas also wants a personal experience. In both his disbelief and his faith, Thomas represents us, the future generations called to believe without having seen Jesus in the flesh.

Jesus invites Thomas to touch the wounds in his risen body. As Jesus and his disciple stand before each other in the midst of the community, it is Thomas's faith, not his hands, that digs deeply into the mystery of his risen Lord, and he cries out the most profound and personal proclamation of gospel faith: "My Lord and my God!" In return, Jesus speaks the greatest of all beatitudes that will resound beyond that Jerusalem room, into our assembly today, and to the end of the ages: "Blessed are those who have not seen and have believed."

✦ How has God invited you to believe without seeing?

Brief Silence

Prayer

Loving God, thank you for the gift of this day and the opportunity to grow in relationship with you. As you breathe your Spirit in us, may we know you without seeing. Open our hearts to your love revealed in manifold ways as we strive to remain faithful to your Gospel and the way of life to which we are called. **Amen**.

In today's gospel Jesus calls his disciples "Children" and cares for them with tender love. May this water remind us of our special relationship with God . . .

Prayer

Persevering God,
though all time you have saved your
      people,
from dangers, sin, death and destruction.
I will praise you, Lord, for you have rescued me.
Let us rest in your protection and safety,
knowing you will never abandon your faithful people.
Amen.

Gospel   **John 21:1-19 (or John 21:1-14)**

At that time, Jesus revealed himself again to his disciples at the Sea of Tiberias. He revealed himself in this way. Together were Simon Peter, Thomas called Didymus, Nathanael from Cana in Galilee, Zebedee's sons, and two others of his disciples. Simon Peter said to them, "I am going fishing." They said to him, "We also will come with you." So they went out and got into the boat, but that night they caught nothing. When it was already dawn, Jesus was standing on the shore; but the disciples did not realize that it was Jesus. Jesus said to them, "Children, have you caught anything to eat?" They answered him, "No." So he said to them, "Cast the net over the right side of the boat and you will find something." So they cast it, and were not able to pull it in because of the number of fish. So the disciple whom Jesus loved said to Peter,

"It is the Lord." When Simon Peter heard that it was the Lord, he tucked in his garment, for he was lightly clad, and jumped into the sea. The other disciples came in the boat, for they were not far from shore, only about a hundred yards, dragging the net with the fish. When they climbed out on shore, they saw a charcoal fire with fish on it and bread. Jesus said to them, "Bring some of the fish you just caught." So Simon Peter went over and dragged the net ashore full of one hundred fifty-three large fish. Even though there were so many, the net was not torn. Jesus said to them, "Come, have breakfast." And none of the disciples dared to ask him, "Who are you?" because they realized it was the Lord. Jesus came over and took the bread and gave it to them, and in like manner the fish. This was now the third time Jesus was revealed to his disciples after being raised from the dead.

When they had finished breakfast, Jesus said to Simon Peter, "Simon, son of John, do you love me more than these?" Simon Peter answered him, "Yes, Lord, you know that I love you." Jesus said to him, "Feed my lambs." He then said to Simon Peter a second time, "Simon, son of John, do you love me?" Simon Peter answered him, "Yes, Lord, you know that I love you." Jesus said to him, "Tend my sheep." Jesus said to him the third time, "Simon, son of John, do you love me?" Peter was distressed that Jesus had said to him a third time, "Do you love me?" and he said to him, "Lord, you know everything; you know that I love you." Jesus said to him, "Feed my sheep. Amen, amen, I say to you, when you were younger, you used to dress yourself and go where you wanted; but when you grow old, you will stretch out your hands, and someone else will dress you and lead you where you do not want to go." He said this signifying by what kind of death he would glorify God. And when he had said this, he said to him, "Follow me."

Brief Silence

For Reflection

The gospel begins as a night scene of failure, with no fish caught. Then the sun rises, and the disciples are hailed from the shore by someone who calls them "[c]hildren." They are the "children" of

John 13:33 who are loved but still have much to learn. The stranger tells them to let down their nets, and emptiness is filled with a great catch. Then with the sun rising and the dawn of faith breaking, the disciple whom Jesus loves, who rested his head on the heart of Jesus, who stood his ground at the cross and holds the preeminent place of intimate contemplation giving him the keen eyes of faith, sees and proclaims with deference to Peter: "It is the Lord." It is Peter, the model for pastoral leadership, but leadership that is also dependent on contemplative insight, who plunges into the water. Always eager and impetuous, he makes his way to Jesus. Again we are reminded that the way to the risen Lord is through the waters, through the baptism into which we are plunged.

✦ Have you ever failed at something so badly, you couldn't possibly try it again? Viewing Peter's transformation through this framework of overcoming what appears to be total failure, can you imagine a situation in which you might revisit your "failed" work?

Brief Silence

Prayer

Loving God, thank you for the gift of this day and the opportunity to grow in relationship with you. You, the author of friendship, offer us friendship. May the relationship between Jesus and the disciples inspire us to grow in relationship as we work to remain faithful to your Gospel and the way of life to which we are called. **Amen**.

In today's gospel we encounter
Christ, the Good Shepherd.
May this water remind us
whose we are . . .

Prayer

Ever-living God,
we call your son "Good Shepherd,"
he who lays down his life for his sheep.
We are his people, the sheep of his flock.
May we ever be mindful that our savior
is also our protection,
he who is Christ, our Lord.
Amen.

Gospel   **John 10:27-30**

Jesus said: "My sheep hear my voice; I know them, and they
follow me. I give them eternal life, and they shall never perish.
No one can take them out of my hand. My Father, who has given
them to me, is greater than all, and no one can take them out of
the Father's hand. The Father and I are one."

Brief Silence

For Reflection

In today's gospel Jesus is speaking in the portico of Solomon's
temple during the winter feast of the Dedication (Hanukkah),
which commemorates God's deliverance of Israel from the Syrian
tyrant, Antiochus Epiphanes. Jesus is not the powerful political
leader that many, with Israel again under occupation, were waiting for, a messiah to save them from civil tyranny. Jesus offers the

people a different security: the safety of eternal life if they commit their lives into his hands and obey his voice. Jesus can do this because the Father has given him the flock for its safekeeping and shepherding. The Easter Triduum tells us how costly Jesus's care of his flock will be, but the body of the Shepherd that is ravaged in death is also raised in glory to know and name his sheep and call them into a share of that glory. With the responsorial Psalm 100 we profess our faith in this and recognize ourselves as belonging to God as his flock. That God's steadfast love endures for us forever is most clearly revealed in the Christ who is both compassionate Shepherd and obedient Lamb.

The voice of the Shepherd is heard now in that of his disciples.

✦ Who or what do you follow? Material success? Professional gain? Social acclaim? How can you reorient yourself to Christ, the Good Shepherd?

Brief Silence

Prayer
Loving God, thank you for the gift of this day and the opportunity to grow in relationship with you. Just as a shepherd knows his or her sheep, you intimately know each of us. May we turn away from self-deceit to follow you as we work to remain faithful to your Gospel and the way of life to which we are called. **Amen**.

In today's gospel Jesus calls us to love others as he has loved us. May this water remind us of our call to live in God's love . . .

Prayer

God who Reigns,
above any other name is yours,
majestic and eternal.
I will praise your name forever, my king and my God.
Rule over us as a servant who,
by humility and without pretention,
leads by the example of love and sacrifice.
Amen.

Gospel   **John 13:31-33a, 34-35**

When Judas had left them, Jesus said, "Now is the Son of Man glorified, and God is glorified in him. If God is glorified in him, God will also glorify him in himself, and God will glorify him at once. My children, I will be with you only a little while longer. I give you a new commandment: love one another. As I have loved you, so you also should love one another. This is how all will know that you are my disciples, if you have love for one another."

Brief Silence

For Reflection

The loss of faith that so often results from the lack of a witness of radical love of one another by believers is tragically evident in the church's past and present. Sexual, physical, or psychological abuse by those called Christian—and especially those in whom great trust has been placed—denominational division and bickering, human rights ignored or violated: all these are failure in obedience to Jesus's command to love one another as he has loved us.

One of the significant New Testament words for resurrection is *anastasis*, "standing up." Jesus stood up for the insignificant, dispossessed, and disadvantaged people; he stood up against the lack of love in powerful people and places, both civil and religious, and he died because this is the way he lived. This is why God "stood up" for Jesus by raising him to the glory of his resurrection. In our parish communities, we may have wonderful liturgies and eager ministers, but if there is also jealousy, possessiveness, status seeking, and more judgment passed than love given by both laity and clergy, if there are subtle policies of exclusion rather than inclusion, shadows fall over us. We become death-dealing individuals rather than life-giving communities.

✦ What is one concrete example of Jesus's love for you in your life?

Brief Silence

Prayer

Loving God, thank you for the gift of this day and the opportunity to grow in relationship with you. May we be known not by our accolades or accomplishments, but by the very real ways we share your love with others. In this same love may we remain faithful to your Gospel and the way of life to which we are called. **Amen**.

Today Jesus tells us, "Peace I leave with you; my peace I give to you." May these waters remind us of the peace for which we live and long . . .

Prayer

O God,
every nation, every tongue shall worship you,
let all the nations praise you!
You are just and equitable,
worthy of worship and of reverence and awe.
Teach us your ways, surpassing all human understanding.
We make this prayer through Christ, our Risen Lord.
Amen.

Gospel   John 14:23-29

Jesus said to his disciples: "Whoever loves me will keep my word, and my Father will love him, and we will come to him and make our dwelling with him. Whoever does not love me does not keep my words; yet the word you hear is not mine but that of the Father who sent me.

"I have told you this while I am with you. The Advocate, the Holy Spirit, whom the Father will send in my name, will teach you everything and remind you of all that I told you. Peace I leave with you; my peace I give to you. Not as the world gives do I give it to you. Do not let your hearts be troubled or afraid. You heard me tell you, 'I am going away and I will come back to you.' If you loved me, you would rejoice that I am going to the Father; for the

Father is greater than I. And now I have told you this before it happens, so that when it happens you may believe."

Brief Silence

For Reflection

On this night of gifts, Jesus offers to his disciples the gift of peace. As with the new love commandment we heard in last week's gospel reading, this peace is also new; it is not sentimental, complacent, secure, or conflict-free because it is, Jesus says, "my peace"—a peace that comforts the afflicted and afflicts the comfortable. It is a gift given not in the context of cozy table talk, but on the cold eve of his death, when one friend has already become an enemy and left the companionship of the table, and Jesus is saying his last goodbyes to those who, with one exception, will fail to stand by him during his passion and death. He assures them that they should not be afraid but find new courage in his peace. This peace is shalom, the right relationship that flows from our loving union with God through Jesus and the Holy Spirit. The Holy Spirit makes connections, establishes unlikely partnerships, and breaks down barriers between people—if we are open and welcoming to the Spirit's advocacy for this in us.

✦ Which areas of your life are in greatest need of peace? How can you continue to invite the Holy Spirit into these areas?

Brief Silence

Prayer

Loving God, thank you for the gift of this day and the opportunity to grow in relationship with you. You offer us the gift of your peace. May we graciously accept this peace into our hearts and readily share it with others as we remain faithful to your Gospel and the way of life to which we are called. **Amen**.

As we celebrate the ascension, Jesus tells his disciples in today's gospel that they are called to give witness by their lives. May these waters strengthen our witness in Christ . . .

Prayer

God of the Great Commission,
you reign from on high yet dwell within each human heart.
To shouts of joy and *a blare of trumpets*
we will acclaim your greatness and sing your praises.
Help us respond to your call with joy and a willing spirit.
Amen.

Gospel   **Luke 24:46-53**

Jesus said to his disciples: "Thus it is written that the Christ would suffer and rise from the dead on the third day and that repentance, for the forgiveness of sins, would be preached in his name to all the nations, beginning from Jerusalem. You are witnesses of these things. And behold I am sending the promise of my Father upon you; but stay in the city until you are clothed with power from on high."

Then he led them out as far as Bethany, raised his hands, and blessed them. As he blessed them he parted from them and was taken up to heaven. They did him homage and then returned to Jerusalem with great joy, and they were continually in the temple praising God.

Brief Silence

For Reflection

As children (and perhaps still as adults, if we take the time) we may have often been fascinated to watch the clouds and see how quickly they formed new shapes, new "pictures," especially on windy days. Above us there seemed to be a "becoming world" of surprises, where nothing was fixed or static. The cloud that is described as enveloping Jesus at his Ascension wraps him in the glory of God and reveals, even as it hides, another aspect of the Beloved Son: that there is no place for his disciples to just look "intently at the sky" (as the first reading puts it). The words of the two messengers who spoke to the apostles after Jesus ascended, men whose dress and words remind us of the two angels at the Resurrection tomb, suggest that this is the wrong kind of waiting, a dawdling that will never harvest the fruits of Jesus's resurrection. The time for eye-witnessing is past; now is the time for proclamation. The Ascension points to the need for Pentecost and the driving, Spirit-filled passion that will make the disciples the witnesses of Jesus throughout the world until he comes again.

✦ What does the kingdom of God look like to you? How do you continue to bring about God's kingdom in your own life?

Brief Silence

Prayer

Loving God, thank you for the gift of this day and the opportunity to grow in relationship with you. You ascend on high, yet are still close to us, inviting us to glorify you through our lives. May our witness be constant as we remain faithful to your Gospel and the way of life to which we are called. **Amen**.

Today Jesus prays that all may know the love of the Father. May this water remind us of God's immense love for us . . .

Prayer

Sovereign God,
you are *the most high over all the earth.*
None are like you, benevolent judge and glorious God.
Your reign is one of sacrifice and love,
your crown is of thorns and your throne a cross.
Let all rejoice and exalt your holy name.
Amen.

Gospel   **John 17:20-26**

Lifting up his eyes to heaven, Jesus prayed, saying: "Holy Father, I pray not only for them, but also for those who will believe in me through their word, so that they may all be one, as you, Father, are in me and I in you, that they also may be in us, that the world may believe that you sent me. And I have given them the glory you gave me, so that they may be one, as we are one, I in them and you in me, that they may be brought to perfection as one, that the world may know that you sent me, and that you loved them even as you loved me. Father, they are your gift to me. I wish that where I am they also may be with me, that they may see my glory that you gave me, because you loved me before the foundation of the world. Righteous Father, the world also does not know you, but I know you, and they know that you sent me.

I made known to them your name and I will make it known, that the love with which you loved me may be in them and I in them."

Brief Silence

For Reflection

The ritual celebration and storytelling of the season of Easter give us an opportunity to reflect deeply on our union with God as we celebrate the fulfillment of that union through Jesus's glorious death, resurrection, and the gift of the hope of an eternal glory that he has given to us. In the gospel reading, Jesus's prayer for unity between God and humankind reveals the main features of the story of our salvation—namely, God becoming human so that God will renew humanity from within, from participation in human life in order to elevate humanity to the status that we share with God.

Another important feature of Jesus's prayer for us is that the love of God, which Jesus Christ experienced in his life and death on the cross, may also be experienced by believers. Jesus is among us as God made flesh manifesting the love of God in his ministry of calling our attention to the presence of God in the world. Christian love originates in God loving us first, and God's love for us is manifested in the self-giving of Jesus Christ on the cross.

✦ When in your life do you feel that you are a gift to others? What are some moments or tasks you remember in which you were being a gift to those around you?

Brief Silence

Prayer

Loving God, thank you for the gift of this day and the opportunity to grow in relationship with you. Your tender love is evident when you speak to us, and you shower us with gifts beyond compare. May we use our gifts for the service of others in your name as we remain faithful to your Gospel and the way of life to which we are called. **Amen**.

On this Pentecost Sunday we celebrate the coming of the Holy Spirit and Jesus entrusting his mission to his apostles then and to us today. May this water remind us of our call and mission . . .

Prayer

Lord,
you bring refreshment and new life to all creation.
We need you, your presence, your vivification.
Send out your Spirit, and renew the face of the earth.
Renew it with justice, equity, and fairness,
and fill it with love, mercy, and truth.
Amen.

Gospel   **John 20:19-23 (or John 14:15-16, 23b-26)**

On the evening of that first day of the week, when the doors were locked, where the disciples were, for fear of the Jews, Jesus came and stood in their midst and said to them, "Peace be with you." When he had said this, he showed them his hands and his side. The disciples rejoiced when they saw the Lord. Jesus said to them again, "Peace be with you. As the Father has sent me, so I send you." And when he had said this, he breathed on them and said to them, "Receive the Holy Spirit. Whose sins you forgive are forgiven them, and whose sins you retain are retained."

Brief Silence

For Reflection

It could be argued that the presence or the anointing of the Holy Spirit is an essential ingredient at the beginning of ministry and for its success. Just as Jesus began his public ministry after being imbued (filled) with the power of the Spirit, the disciples, newly reconstituted as twelve, were told to journey to Jerusalem, where they would receive "power" when the Holy Spirit came upon them. Now that Jesus had physically departed, it was important that the disciples receive the power of the Holy Spirit as they began public ministry as the apostles in Jesus's stead.

Through the sacrament of confirmation, we, too, are "sealed" with the Spirit, which prepares and strengthens us for ministry, our service to the Body of Christ. Pentecost is often viewed as the birth of the church. Pentecost Sunday serves as a reminder of the gift of God's Spirit, bestowed so that we may have power for service and the gift of guidance from the Advocate who will remind us of all truth and be with us always.

✦ Knowing that the first act of the Holy Spirit when sent to the apostles is the work of communication, how can you renew the way you speak with family, friends, and colleagues?

Brief Silence

Prayer

Loving God, thank you for the gift of this day and the opportunity to grow in relationship with you. Your presence is known by the gift of your Spirit, the Advocate that is with us now and always. May we cultivate our awareness of your Spirit with intentionality as we remain faithful to your Gospel and the way of life to which we are called. **Amen.**

As we celebrate the Most Holy Trinity, we delve deeper into the relationship between the Father, Son, and Holy Spirit. We, too, are called to participate in this relationship. For the times we have failed to live as we are called, we ask the triune God for pardon and peace . . .

Prayer

O God,
you are three in one, a divine community:
how wonderful your name in all the earth!
You imbue all creation as relationship and community;
keep us ever in that communion with each other and with you,
who live and reign as one God, for ever and ever.
Amen.

Gospel   **John 16:12-15**

Jesus said to his disciples: "I have much more to tell you, but you cannot bear it now. But when he comes, the Spirit of truth, he will guide you to all truth. He will not speak on his own, but he will speak what he hears, and will declare to you the things that are coming. He will glorify me, because he will take from what is mine and declare it to you. Everything that the Father has is mine; for this reason I told you that he will take from what is mine and declare it to you."

Brief Silence

For Reflection

Theology has developed a word to describe the dynamic relation-ship between the Persons of the Trinity and the community of believers—*perichoresis*, or "dance." In this metaphorical language, the Trinity is a partnership of encircling and embracing, a graceful movement of loving attentiveness into which we are invited as partners who must, in our turn, draw others into the dance by our loving outreach to them. With the imagery of the dance we cannot think of God as solitary.

Theology, preaching, metaphor may all help towards some understanding of who and what we celebrate on this feast, but perhaps it is again the poet who has the insight to realize that it is only in the communion of death, when we are drawn into the community of those whom the poet George Herbert calls the "unnumbered Three," that we will truly see and understand because it is only then, in death, that the dust we are will be transformed. No longer will it blow into our eyes to blind us, but it will become a seeing dust that sparkles with a revelation of the mystery of the Three in our mutually unveiled presence.

✦ When have you seen God revealed in relationship and community? What do these experiences teach you about the nature of the Trinity?

Brief Silence

Prayer

Loving God, thank you for the gift of this day and the opportunity to grow in relationship with you. Your very essence is relationship. Draw us more fully into relationship with you, that we might know how to live with and for others as we remain faithful to your Gospel and the way of life to which we are called. **Amen**.

Nourished by God in Word and sacrament, we take a moment to recall the times we have failed to follow Christ's example in our lives, asking for peace and healing . . .

Prayer

God of All,
you call us to a sacred vocation,
and together to the priesthood of the baptized.
Together with the priesthood of the ordained, you remind us:
"You are a priest forever, in the line of Melchizedek."
Bless our ministries with fruitfulness and joy.
Amen.

Gospel   **Luke 9:11b-17**

Jesus spoke to the crowds about the kingdom of God, and he healed those who needed to be cured. As the day was drawing to a close, the Twelve approached him and said, "Dismiss the crowd so that they can go to the surrounding villages and farms and find lodging and provisions; for we are in a deserted place here." He said to them, "Give them some food yourselves." They replied, "Five loaves and two fish are all we have, unless we ourselves go and buy food for all these people." Now the men there numbered about five thousand. Then he said to his disciples, "Have them sit down in groups of about fifty." They did so and made them all sit down. Then taking the five loaves and the two fish, and looking up to heaven, he said the blessing over them, broke them, and gave them to the disciples to set before the crowd. They all ate and were satisfied. And when the leftover fragments were picked up, they filled twelve wicker baskets.

Brief Silence

For Reflection

The Twelve tell Jesus to send the crowd away to find shelter and food, neither of which is available in the lonely place, but Jesus challenges them: "Give them some food yourselves." Having just completed their first missionary field work, the apostles are now called to partnership with Jesus in another apostolic mission: feeding hungry crowds.

Jesus's command that the Twelve seat the crowd in a hundred groups of fifty each is an image of the local churches gathered as the church universal. Just as Jesus has taught the crowd throughout the day, so he will now teach his disciples about the kingdom in action when he takes, blesses, breaks, and gives the five loaves and two fishes into the hands of the disciples to give to the crowd.

Luke obviously wants his community, and all hearers of the gospel, to connect this meal with the feeding traditions of his ancestors: the miraculous manna in the wilderness (Exod 16:15) and the story of Elisha who fed a smaller crowd with loaves of bread, some of which were left over (2 Kgs 4:42-44). Into this past, the present of the gospel Bethsaida and all our eucharistic "Bethsaidas" are gathered.

✦ What are your own experiences of breaking bread with others? Why are these opportunities so significant?

Brief Silence

Prayer

Loving God, thank you for the gift of this day and the opportunity to grow in relationship with you. You yourself are gift to us, and you provide for our every need beyond compare. Take all anxiety from our hearts and fill us with your peace as we remain faithful to your Gospel and the way of life to which we are called. **Amen**.

Jesus invites each of us to follow him. For the times we have not followed Christ in our thoughts, words, and actions, we ask for God's healing and forgiveness . . .

Prayer

Ever-present God,
there are times when the world seems bleak,
and friends and family seem distant.
Help us to remember, in the darkness,
that *you are our inheritance, O Lord.*
You are generous with your love and presence,
and never far from those who seek you.
Amen.

Gospel

Luke 9:51-62

When the days for Jesus' being taken up were fulfilled, he resolutely determined to journey to Jerusalem, and he sent messengers ahead of him. On the way they entered a Samaritan village to prepare for his reception there, but they would not welcome him because the destination of his journey was Jerusalem. When the disciples James and John saw this they asked, "Lord, do you want us to call down fire from heaven to consume them?" Jesus turned and rebuked them, and they journeyed to another village.

As they were proceeding on their journey someone said to him, "I will follow you wherever you go." Jesus answered him, "Foxes have dens and birds of the sky have nests, but the Son of Man has nowhere to rest his head."

And to another he said, "Follow me." But he replied, "Lord, let me go first and bury my father." But he answered him, "Let the dead bury their dead. But you, go and proclaim the kingdom of

God." And another said, "I will follow you, Lord, but first let me say farewell to my family at home." To him Jesus said, "No one who sets a hand to the plow and looks to what was left behind is fit for the kingdom of God."

Brief Silence

For Reflection

The third of three would-be disciples in today's gospel reading wants to follow Jesus, but on condition that he is allowed to "first say farewell to my family at home." This seems a reasonable request, especially in the light of the first reading that describes how Elijah gave Elisha permission to go and say goodbye. But the following of Jesus has to be unswerving; not even this detour is allowed. The mini-parable of the plow explains further what is also Luke's literary device of exaggeration. The light Palestinian plow was guided with one hand, usually the left, while the plower's other hand carried a stick with which to goad the oxen that pulled the plow. To make a furrow that was straight and of the right depth, to lift the plow over rocks that might shatter it, demanded great concentration and dexterity. To take one's eyes off the plow for a moment could spell disaster. So it is with his disciples, says Jesus. The eyes of our heart must be fixed on the reign of God with unwavering commitment so that the field of this world may be well plowed and made ready for God's harvesting.

✦ How do you balance looking toward the future while still being mindful of the reality of the present?

Brief Silence

Prayer

Loving God, thank you for the gift of this day and the opportunity to grow in relationship with you. Help us keep our eyes on the plough, ever looking toward you, the source of our salvation. Guide us as we strive to remain faithful to your Gospel and the way of life to which we are called. **Amen.**

Jesus sends us out to follow his example and love in his name. For the times we have not loved as we should, we ask for God's forgiveness . . .

Prayer

Miraculous God,
time and again you break into human time and space
to save your people and show your might.
Let all the earth cry out to you, shouting praise!
Help us to always see your deeds among us,
you who are still active and present in our lives.
Amen.

Gospel   Luke 10:1-12, 17-20 (or Luke 10:1-9)

At that time the Lord appointed seventy-two others whom he sent ahead of him in pairs to every town and place he intended to visit. He said to them, "The harvest is abundant but the laborers are few; so ask the master of the harvest to send out laborers for his harvest. Go on your way; behold, I am sending you like lambs among wolves. Carry no money bag, no sack, no sandals; and greet no one along the way. Into whatever house you enter, first say, 'Peace to this household.' If a peaceful person lives there, your peace will rest on him; but if not, it will return to you. Stay in the same house and eat and drink what is offered to you, for the laborer deserves his payment. Do not move about from one house to another. Whatever town you enter and they welcome you, eat what is set before you, cure the sick in it and say to them, 'The kingdom of God is at hand for you.' Whatever town you enter and they do not receive you, go out into the streets and say, 'The dust of your town that clings to our feet, even that we shake off against you.' Yet know this: the kingdom of God is at hand. I tell you, it will be more tolerable for Sodom on that day than for that town."

The seventy-two returned rejoicing, and said, "Lord, even the demons are subject to us because of your name." Jesus said, "I have observed Satan fall like lightning from the sky. Behold, I have given you the power to 'tread upon serpents' and scorpions and upon the full force of the enemy and nothing will harm you. Nevertheless, do not rejoice because the spirits are subject to you, but rejoice because your names are written in heaven."

Brief Silence

For Reflection

"Mission statements" are important for organizations of all kinds. Luke presents today's gospel as the early church's "mission statement" and a practical handbook for its implementation. How can we distill the essence of its truth to inform our mission today?

First, the world needs the mission of Christians because there is a plentiful harvest waiting to be reaped. Second, prayer to "the master of the harvest" is essential for the empowering of the harvesters. Third, because it is Jesus who sends us on mission, we can go in confidence in his active protection. This is not to discount the fourth missionary principle: the reminder that there are "wolves" to be confronted on the way—personal, communal, and structural realities that will try to hunt down and consume those who proclaim the Gospel. Every generation of Christians needs the gift of discernment so that we can name and recognize these "wolves." Finally, when the goal of our journey is the reign of God, money, possessions (or perhaps possessiveness), or concern with status can be hindering baggage. "Carry nothing" is again a device of exaggeration that would have been understood by Luke's communities as emphasizing the urgency of the mission.

✦ What baggage (material, personal, social, etc.) prevents you from focusing fully on the presence of God in your life? If necessary, how might you reevaluate some of your priorities?

Brief Silence

Prayer

Loving God, thank you for the gift of this day and the opportunity to grow in relationship with you. As you model hospitality for us may we extend that same hospitality to others. Offering a plentiful welcome to all, may we remain faithful to your Gospel and the way of life to which we are called. **Amen**.

Today we hear the parable of the Good Samaritan. For the times we have failed to love as we are called, we ask God for healing and forgiveness . . .

Prayer

God of the Covenants,
through all ages, your prophets spoke
    truth
to those who had forgotten your ways:
Turn to the Lord in your need, and you will live.
Help us to know when we stray from your path,
and to return to you with our whole hearts.
Amen.

Gospel   Luke 10:25-37

There was a scholar of the law who stood up to test Jesus and said, "Teacher, what must I do to inherit eternal life?" Jesus said to him, "What is written in the law? How do you read it?" He said in reply, *"You shall love the Lord, your God, with all your heart, with all your being, with all your strength, and with all your mind, and your neighbor as yourself."* He replied to him, "You have answered correctly; do this and you will live."

But because he wished to justify himself, he said to Jesus, "And who is my neighbor?" Jesus replied, "A man fell victim to robbers as he went down from Jerusalem to Jericho. They stripped and beat him and went off leaving him half-dead. A priest happened to be going down that road, but when he saw him, he passed by on the opposite side. Likewise a Levite came to the place, and when he saw him, he passed by on the opposite side. But a Samaritan traveler who came upon him was moved with compassion at the sight. He approached the victim, poured oil and wine over his wounds and bandaged them. Then he lifted him up on his own animal, took him to an inn, and cared for him. The next day he took out two silver coins and gave them to the innkeeper with the instruction, 'Take care of him. If you spend more than what I have given you, I shall repay you on my way back.' Which of these three, in your opinion, was neighbor to the robbers' victim?" He answered, "The one who treated him with mercy." Jesus said to him, "Go and do likewise."

Brief Silence

For Reflection

The parable of the Good Samaritan is a "shocking" story, intended to make us think about alternatives in our relationships with God and one another. It is introduced with the lawyer's determined effort to justify himself with regard to the two great commandments: love of God and love of neighbor. "[W]hat must *I* do to inherit eternal life?" he asks, and Jesus responds with two questions: "What is written in the law? How do you read it?" The lawyer is quick to answer; he has all the right and holy words, can quote his source documents perfectly. But Jesus urges him from right answering to right living: "[D]o this and you will live."

But the lawyer continues to seek after self-justification rather than truth, responding: "And who is *my* neighbor?" Everything is in reference to himself. But discipleship does not start with asking, what are the boundaries of my responsibility? Jesus asks, "Which of these three, in your opinion, was neighbor to the robbers' victim?" This is how our commitment to Jesus is to be defined: from the perspective of the half-dead, the fallen, the wounded, the abandoned ones.

✦ Have you ever ignored or sidestepped a person or issue because you were uncomfortable?

Brief Silence

Prayer

Loving God, thank you for the gift of this day and the opportunity to grow in relationship with you. There are no strangers with you, only beloved brothers and sisters on a common journey. Quell our fears and give us confidence to respond to you, that we may remain faithful to your Gospel and the way of life to which we are called. **Amen**.

In today's gospel we hear of Martha and Mary and their love for Jesus. For the times we have not loved God and others as we should, we ask for forgiveness . . .

Prayer

Divine Righteousness,
you teach us to walk uprightly, and with integrity.
When one *does justice*,
the presence of the Lord abides with us more fully,
and all live together in peace and harmony.
Be always with us, and bring your justice to birth among us.
Amen.

Gospel   **Luke 10:38-42**

Jesus entered a village where a woman whose name was Martha welcomed him. She had a sister named Mary who sat beside the Lord at his feet listening to him speak. Martha, burdened with much serving, came to him and said, "Lord, do you not care that my sister has left me by myself to do the serving? Tell her to help me." The Lord said to her in reply, "Martha, Martha, you are anxious and worried about many things. There is need of only one thing. Mary has chosen the better part and it will not be taken from her."

Brief Silence

For Reflection

When Jesus arrives at Mary and Martha's house, Martha emerges as the dominant sister: the house is described as her home; she is the one who "welcomed" him; Mary is her sister. What distracts Martha is her service, her *diakonia*, a word that in the early church had a much broader meaning than only domestic duties. She complains that Mary's sitting silently at Jesus's feet is no help to her ministry. Rather like the lawyer in last week's parable, Martha is indulging in self-justification.

In response, Jesus admonishes her. Mary has chosen the better part on this occasion, but for both the sisters it is only a *part* of the service of Jesus, not the whole picture; nor is the service of Jesus constant or unwavering by either sister. Only both sisters, together, can accommodate Jesus in the way he should be welcomed.

We don't have to choose once and for all between contemplation and action. Rather, we can and should welcome both, respect our differences, and accept that we may be sometimes one and sometimes the other.

✦ How do you tend to show hospitality? Likewise, how do you receive the hospitality offered by someone else?

Brief Silence

Prayer

Loving God, thank you for the gift of this day and the opportunity to grow in relationship with you. Increase in us our awareness to celebrate your presence in all aspects of our daily interactions. May we show and receive love, following your example that we may remain faithful to your Gospel and the way of life to which we are called. **Amen**.

In the Lord's Prayer, we call on God to forgive us our sins just as we forgive those who have wronged us. For the times we have sinned or failed to extend forgiveness, we ask for God's healing and peace . . .

Prayer

Lord,

you are an ever-present help, and constant friend.

On the day [we] called for help, you answered [us].

Be with us now, that when someone needs our help,

We may show them your compassion, kindness, and love,

you who live and reign for ever and ever.

Amen.

Gospel   Luke 11:1-13

Jesus was praying in a certain place, and when he had finished, one of his disciples said to him, "Lord, teach us to pray just as John taught his disciples." He said to them, "When you pray, say: / Father, hallowed be your name, / your kingdom come. / Give us each day our daily bread / and forgive us our sins / for we ourselves forgive everyone in debt to us, / and do not subject us to the final test."

And he said to them, "Suppose one of you has a friend to whom he goes at midnight and says, 'Friend, lend me three loaves of bread, for a friend of mine has arrived at my house from a journey and I have nothing to offer him,' and he says in reply from within, 'Do not bother me; the door has already been locked and my children and I are already in bed. I cannot get up to give you anything.' I tell you, if he does not get up to give the visitor the loaves because of their friendship, he will get up to give him whatever he needs because of his persistence.

"And I tell you, ask and you will receive; seek and you will find; knock and the door will be opened to you. For everyone who asks, receives; and the one who seeks, finds; and to the one who knocks, the door will be opened. What father among you would hand his son a snake when he asks for a fish? Or hand him a scorpion when he asks for an egg? If you then, who are wicked, know how to give good gifts to your children, how much more will the Father in heaven give the Holy Spirit to those who ask him?"

Brief Silence

For Reflection

Our familiarity with the Lord's Prayer may blunt our appreciation of its radical, even subversive, teaching about prayer. It is to be the prayer of a community that is conscious both of its intimate relationship with God and its presence in and responsibility for the world. In both Testaments, God is "Father," a metaphor vastly different from that of the powerful Roman emperor, the "father of the homeland," or the authoritarian father of the family social unit. Especially in the gospels, God is the Abba of Jesus, in loving, faithful, and intimate relationship with the Beloved Son.

The kingdom for which disciples pray is not a kingdom of political power, but one that belongs to the poor, the liberated, excluded women, forgiven sinners. That we may be changed, we pray for bread, forgiveness, and deliverance. Given Luke's emphasis on hospitality, prayer for "our daily bread" is probably a request for this basic necessity that should be shared with the poor. We also need to be nourished with one another's forgiveness, because God will never starve us of forgiveness, and God's behavior must be the norm for his sons and daughters.

✦ Why do you pray?

Brief Silence

Prayer

Loving God, thank you for the gift of this day and the opportunity to grow in relationship with you. You teach us that prayer is both personal and communal. May we dare to bring the realities of our world to our prayer that we may remain faithful to your Gospel and the way of life to which we are called. **Amen.**

In today's gospel Jesus warns us to guard ourselves against greed. For the times we have been greedy in our thoughts, words, and actions, we ask for God's healing forgiveness and restorative peace . . .

Prayer

Eternal God,
you continually call us to conversion,
and bid us, *"harden not your hearts."*
Give us ears to listen, to hear your voice,
and may our hearts be moved
to return to you with a contrite spirit.
Amen.

Gospel   **Luke 12:13-21**

Someone in the crowd said to Jesus, "Teacher, tell my brother to share the inheritance with me." He replied to him, "Friend, who appointed me as your judge and arbitrator?" Then he said to the crowd, "Take care to guard against all greed, for though one may be rich, one's life does not consist of possessions."

Then he told them a parable. "There was a rich man whose land produced a bountiful harvest. He asked himself, 'What shall I do, for I do not have space to store my harvest?' And he said, 'This is what I shall do: I shall tear down my barns and build larger ones. There I shall store all my grain and other goods and I shall say to myself, "Now as for you, you have so many good things stored up for many years, rest, eat, drink, be merry!"' But God said to him, 'You fool, this night your life will be demanded of you; and the things you have prepared, to whom will they belong?' Thus will it be for all who store up treasure for themselves but are not rich in what matters to God."

Brief Silence

For Reflection

The man, the "fool," in Jesus's parable today is rich, with a surplus harvest. He has no appreciation that this blessing is from God, nor of the Jewish religious tradition and human prudence that demanded that he make provision for himself and his whole community in case of any famine that might follow years of plenty. His "retirement plan" is a self-centered recital of "I will, I will, I will," well-punctuated by references to "my." The rich man considers that he owns everything: crops, barns, grains, and even his own soul. In a culture where a transaction at a street stall involved long and animated discussion between buyer and seller, the inappropriateness of such self-talk would not be lost on Jesus's audience. Likewise, it was expected that important decisions would be made in community, but for this man there is no one with whom he can or wants to talk—no family, cronies, advisers. His calculated option is to make and live in an isolated and alienating vacuum. This cannot be the option of Jesus's disciples. Life in community and attention to the community's most needy are essential.

✦ How would you define or describe *wealth*?

Brief Silence

Prayer

Loving God, thank you for the gift of this day and the opportunity to grow in relationship with you. Remind us to live and love in the moment, responding to the needs of others without reservation. May we give of ourselves generously as we remain faithful to your Gospel and the way of life to which we are called. **Amen.**

In today's gospel Jesus tells us, "Do not be afraid." For the times we have allowed fear to control our thoughts and actions, we ask for God's healing and peace . . .

Prayer

Divine Compassion,
our eyes look to you, thankful and full of wonder.
Blessed are we, *chosen to be* your own.
May your eyes always be upon us,
for we hope in you, our safety and shield.
Never lose sight of us, as we remain fixed on you.
Amen.

Gospel   Luke 12:32-48 (or Luke 12:35-40)

Jesus said to his disciples: "Do not be afraid any longer, little flock, for your Father is pleased to give you the kingdom. Sell your belongings and give alms. Provide money bags for yourselves that do not wear out, an inexhaustible treasure in heaven that no thief can reach nor moth destroy. For where your treasure is, there also will your heart be.

"Gird your loins and light your lamps and be like servants who await their master's return from a wedding, ready to open immediately when he comes and knocks. Blessed are those servants whom the master finds vigilant on his arrival. Amen, I say to you, he will gird himself, have them recline at table, and proceed to wait on them. And should he come in the second or third watch and find them prepared in this way, blessed are those servants.

Be sure of this: if the master of the house had known the hour when the thief was coming, he would not have let his house be broken into. You also must be prepared, for at an hour you do not expect, the Son of Man will come."

Then Peter said, "Lord, is this parable meant for us or for everyone?" And the Lord replied, "Who, then, is the faithful and prudent steward whom the master will put in charge of his servants to distribute the food allowance at the proper time? Blessed is that servant whom his master on arrival finds doing so. Truly, I say to you, the master will put the servant in charge of all his property. But if that servant says to himself, 'My master is delayed in coming,' and begins to beat the menservants and the maidservants, to eat and drink and get drunk, then that servant's master will come on an unexpected day and at an unknown hour and will punish the servant severely and assign him a place with the unfaithful. That servant who knew his master's will but did not make preparations nor act in accord with his will shall be beaten severely; and the servant who was ignorant of his master's will but acted in a way deserving of a severe beating shall be beaten only lightly. Much will be required of the person entrusted with much, and still more will be demanded of the person entrusted with more."

Brief Silence

For Reflection

The sayings and parables of today's gospel are stitched together with the themes of vigilance, preparedness, and fidelity. Christians are to be "girded," ready for action. The biblical memory behind the parable's action is the Passover from Egypt when the Hebrews had to be girded, clothed, and belted up, ready for their escape into freedom. The early church lived in expectation of Christ's return during the great Easter night, yet unfolding history showed that the watch for the Parousia would be long.

In the first parable, addressed to disciples in general, the faithful servants are eagerly awaiting their master's return from a wedding banquet, a favorite biblical image of the end time. The positioning of it in both the middle of Luke's gospel and halfway through the journey to Jerusalem reminds us to be alert at all times so that we may recognize the Lord when he comes. He comes in those we meet, in the circumstances of our daily lives, and in the signs of our times. In a very real sense, every hour is an hour of the Lord's coming and knocking, and our response to this will either prepare for or hinder its final fulfillment.

✦ Do you ever make excuses for not prioritizing your relationship with God? If so, how might today's gospel reinvigorate you to seek the Lord above all else?

Brief Silence

Prayer

Loving God, thank you for the gift of this day and the opportunity to grow in relationship with you. As we respond to your call to place our treasure in heaven, may we relinquish the burdens of our earthly possessions and priorities. With vigilance, we remain faithful to your Gospel and the way of life to which we are called. **Amen.**

In today's reading from the letter to the Hebrews, we are charged to "rid ourselves of every burden and sin that clings to us." With this, we ask for God's healing and forgiveness . . .

Prayer

God of the Poor and Afflicted,
We stand before you in awe, and in greatest
    need:
come to [our] aid!
Place always on our lips your song,
a melody of wonder and of gratitude.
You are a faithful helper and deliverer, to all
    your holy people.
Amen.

Gospel
Luke 12:49-53

Jesus said to his disciples: "I have come to set the earth on fire, and how I wish it were already blazing! There is a baptism with which I must be baptized, and how great is my anguish until it is accomplished! Do you think that I have come to establish peace on the earth? No, I tell you, but rather division. From now on a household of five will be divided, three against two and two against three; a father will be divided against his son and a son against his father, a mother against her daughter and a daughter against her mother, a mother-in-law against her daughter-in-law and a daughter-in-law against her mother-in-law."

Brief Silence

For Reflection

The inhabitants of Jerusalem would have been familiar with the burning of garbage in the Valley of Gehenna just outside the city.

But there is another and blessed fire that is to be lit from the person of Jesus himself, who burns with a wild love for the world. This is emphasized by the personal repetition in today's passage: "I have come" (said twice), "I wish," "I must be baptized," "I tell you." For Jesus to speak of himself in the first person in the Synoptic Gospels is extremely rare. It is an indication of his urgency. The adult Jesus who is speaking was the child whose birth was announced as heralding peace (Luke 2:14) but was also recognized by Simeon as a source of division (Luke 2:34). The two are not incompatible. Jesus's peace is not a warm, fuzzy glow, a comfortable satisfaction with the status quo. It is a burning decisiveness that results from the self-discovery and discernment that Jesus experienced in the wilderness—that fierce place of temptation and commitment. Out of the wilderness he was driven on mission by the power of the Spirit, ready to live, suffer, and die for the salvation of the world.

✦ How does Jesus call you to "set the world on fire"? How do you respond to this call?

Brief Silence

Prayer
Loving God, thank you for the gift of this day and the opportunity to grow in relationship with you. Following your call is not always easy. Give us the courage to look beyond our own selfish needs and desires to see the needs of others as we work to remain faithful to your Gospel and the way of life to which we are called. **Amen.**

THE ASSUMPTION OF
THE BLESSED VIRGIN MARY

Today on the Assumption we celebrate Mary's life, a life lived in
total service to God and others. For
the times we have not lived as we
are called, we ask for God's healing
and peace . . .

Prayer
God,
you choose the small, weak, and voiceless
to bring your word to both
disconsolate hearts and the proud of heart.
Your vessel, Mary, brought forth your Word
in flesh and bone, and was raised from lowly estate:
the queen stands at your right hand.
May we, like Mary, one day know your eternal glory.
Amen.

Gospel   Luke 1:39-56
Mary set out and traveled to the hill country in haste to a town of
Judah, where she entered the house of Zechariah and greeted
Elizabeth. When Elizabeth heard Mary's greeting, the infant
leaped in her womb, and Elizabeth, filled with the Holy Spirit,
cried out in a loud voice and said, "Blessed are you among women,
and blessed is the fruit of your womb. And how does this happen
to me, that the mother of my Lord should come to me? For at the
moment the sound of your greeting reached my ears, the infant in
my womb leaped for joy. Blessed are you who believed that what
was spoken to you by the Lord would be fulfilled."

And Mary said: / "My soul proclaims the greatness of the
Lord; / my spirit rejoices in God my Savior / for he has looked
with favor on his lowly servant. / From this day all generations
will call me blessed: / the Almighty has done great things for me, /
and holy is his Name. / He has mercy on those who fear him / in
every generation. / He has shown the strength of his arm, / and

has scattered the proud in their conceit. / He has cast down the mighty from their thrones, / and has lifted up the lowly. / He has filled the hungry with good things, / and the rich he has sent away empty. / He has come to the help of his servant Israel / for he has remembered his promise of mercy, / the promise he made to our fathers, / to Abraham and his children forever."

Mary remained with her about three months and then returned to her home.

Brief Silence

For Reflection

When the Blessed Virgin Mary declares in the canticle that she has found favor with God, her experience of God's favor includes protection for her and her child from the murderous scheme of King Herod. God's favor is with her as the prophecy of Simeon pierces her heart with concern for her son. God continues to do great things in her life when she was filled with sorrow for the safety of her child whom she has not seen for three days since the end of the festival in Jerusalem. Sorrow fills her heart at the death of her son, yet God's favor remains for her a source of courage in adversity.

We celebrate her Assumption with the firm belief that her dormition to heaven is the climax of her experience of God's favor. God lifted up the Blessed Mother and gave her the favor of a heavenly home on account of her faithfulness to God. Likewise, our faithfulness to God no matter the circumstances of our life is the sure hope of our own experience of being judged as righteous before God.

✦ Which line of Mary's *Magnificat* particularly resonates with you today? How do these words both challenge and inspire you?

Brief Silence

Prayer

Loving God, thank you for the gift of this day and the opportunity to grow in relationship with you. Like Mary, may we respond to your pressing invitation and contribute to bringing about the completion of creation. May we hold all people as chosen and beloved in your sight as we work to remain faithful to your Gospel and the way of life to which we are called. **Amen**.

In today's gospel Jesus instructs us to strive to enter through the narrow gate. For the times we have rejected this invitation, we ask for healing and forgiveness . . .

Prayer

God of Glory,
we praise your name,
remembering your great works and mighty deeds.
Inspire all of your faithful, mindful of your works,
To *go out to all the world and tell the good news:*
your mercy, your love, and your salvation.
Amen.

Gospel   Luke 13:22-30

Jesus passed through towns and villages, teaching as he went and making his way to Jerusalem. Someone asked him, "Lord, will only a few people be saved?" He answered them, "Strive to enter through the narrow gate, for many, I tell you, will attempt to enter but will not be strong enough. After the master of the house has arisen and locked the door, then will you stand outside knocking and saying, 'Lord, open the door for us.' He will say to you in reply, 'I do not know where you are from.' And you will say, 'We ate and drank in your company and you taught in our streets.' Then he will say to you, 'I do not know where you are from. Depart from me, all you evildoers!' And there will be wailing and grinding of teeth when you see Abraham, Isaac, and Jacob and all the prophets in the kingdom of God and you yourselves cast out.

And people will come from the east and the west and from the north and the south and will recline at table in the kingdom of God. For behold, some are last who will be first, and some are first who will be last."

Brief Silence

For Reflection

"Lord, will only a few be saved?" someone asks Jesus—no doubt with the unspoken hope "along with me!" The anonymity of the questioner drags us all into both the question and Jesus's reply. This reply is not a direct answer, but a parable about the effort that is needed to be saved. Central to the parable is the image of the narrow door. It is not a locked door, but one that requires disciples to give up self-indulgent ways and go into a spiritual training program that will slim us down and enable us to pass through this door into the kingdom. The media is full of stories of the demanding regime that athletes have to follow in their training. To squeeze into a sports team, especially as a representative of one's country, is a cause for celebration; to be citizens who squeeze into the kingdom of God (Phil 3:20) is an eternal joy beyond compare. It is in Jerusalem, where Jesus is heading to suffer, that the narrow door of salvation will be forced sufficiently wide for us by his crucified and risen body.

✦ How do you feel about Jesus's statement, "Strive to enter the narrow gate, for many, I tell you, will attempt to enter but will not be strong enough"?

Brief Silence

Prayer

Loving God, thank you for the gift of this day and the opportunity to grow in relationship with you. May we keep our sight on you alone and strive to enter the narrow gate. Knowing the last and least will be first in your kingdom, may we practice humility as we remain faithful to your Gospel and the way of life to which we are called. **Amen**.

In today's gospel Jesus commands us to humble ourselves, part of which is recognizing our own weaknesses and wounds. For the times we have not been who we are called to be, we ask for God's healing and peace . . .

Prayer

God,

in your goodness, you have made a home for the poor.
Help us, trapped in sins of apathy and greed,
to welcome into our hearts the least among us,
those most in need of sustenance and shelter.
Keep us aware that your body is hurting and needs our help.
Amen.

Gospel   Luke 14:1, 7-14

On a sabbath Jesus went to dine at the home of one of the leading Pharisees, and the people there were observing him carefully.

He told a parable to those who had been invited, noticing how they were choosing the places of honor at the table. "When you are invited by someone to a wedding banquet, do not recline at table in the place of honor. A more distinguished guest than you may have been invited by him, and the host who invited both of you may approach you and say, 'Give your place to this man,' and then you would proceed with embarrassment to take the lowest place. Rather, when you are invited, go and take the lowest place so that when the host comes to you he may say, 'My friend, move up to a higher position.' Then you will enjoy the esteem of your companions at the table. For everyone who exalts himself will be humbled, but the one who humbles himself will be exalted." Then he said to the host who invited him, "When you hold a lunch or a dinner, do not invite your friends or your brothers or your relatives or your wealthy neighbors, in case they may invite you back and you have repayment. Rather, when you hold a banquet, invite the poor, the crippled, the lame, the blind; blessed indeed will you be because of their inability to repay you. For you will be repaid at the resurrection of the righteous."

Brief Silence

For Reflection

Jesus describes how a guest at a wedding banquet loses face when asked by the host to move to a lower place because someone more important has arrived. To presume self-importance is great foolishness. But to be humble is an honorable attitude and is recognized as such by the host's invitation to take a more important place at the table. But the parable is more than a piece of conventional social wisdom. A wedding banquet is frequently a biblical image of the heavenly banquet, and so we can hear this parable as a warning that it will be much more painful if, at the kingdom banquet, we find ourselves put down for those who had no such grandiose opinions of themselves. Those who are most distinguished in God's eyes may be the very ones whom we blindly consider to be of little worth. What we do "now" is preparing for our "not yet" reception in God's house. In our contemporary situation, it is not so much the grab for seats at a meal, but the 'wannabe' culture that, in so many contexts, tempts us to elbow others out as we try to climb the ladder of self-importance and success.

✦ Who do you exclude, either intentionally or unintentionally, from your home, church, and community? How does today's gospel inspire you to sow seeds of inclusion rather than the weeds of "otherness"?

Brief Silence

Prayer

Loving God, thank you for the gift of this day and the opportunity to grow in relationship with you. You show us how to choose humility over exultation, vulnerability over power, and unity over exclusion. May we be willing to dine with all people, especially those who have been relegated to the margins: people who are poor and hurting and grieving and ill, for in doing so we remain faithful to your Gospel and the way of life to which we are called. **Amen**.

In today's gospel Jesus tells us that we must carry our crosses and follow after him. For the times we have rejected Christ's gift of self-love, we ask for forgiveness and healing . . .

Prayer

O Lord,
you are Alpha and Omega, beginning and end.
In every age, you have been our refuge.
Teach us to know our limits, and to trust in you.
Show us your care and wisdom,
that we may be filled with your kindness all our days.
Amen.

Gospel
Luke 14:25-33

Great crowds were traveling with Jesus, and he turned and addressed them, "If anyone comes to me without hating his father and mother, wife and children, brothers and sisters, and even his own life, he cannot be my disciple. Whoever does not carry his own cross and come after me cannot be my disciple. Which of you wishing to construct a tower does not first sit down and calculate the cost to see if there is enough for its completion? Otherwise, after laying the foundation and finding himself unable to finish the work the onlookers should laugh at him and say, 'This one began to build but did not have the resources to finish.' Or what king marching into battle would not first sit down and decide whether with ten thousand troops he can successfully oppose another king advancing upon him with twenty thousand troops? But if not, while he is still far away, he will send a delegation to ask for peace terms. In the same way, anyone of you who does not renounce all his possessions cannot be my disciple."

Brief Silence

For Reflection

The first foolish man is a landowner who decides to build a tower, probably a watchtower, on his property. He is a captive of his wild, momentary enthusiasms. He wants a tower; let there be a tower! But he has no finances to raise anything on the foundations except the ridicule of the onlookers who scoff at his lack of foresight and planning. The other man is the king who engages in the serious business of war. He would be a fool not to weigh the possibilities of succeeding with a smaller army than his opponent and try to negotiate for peace rather than engage in war. As builder and king, both the men are people of some substance, so to fail in what they set out to do will be a cause of great shame. Jesus seems to suggest that it is disciples who have some material and social means at their disposal who need to consider the cost of discipleship most carefully, because they will pay a greater price in terms of social status and possessions if they give up these to follow him. Today's gospel is a source of both encouragement and challenge.

✦ What do you find is the most difficult part about following Christ? Why?

Brief Silence

Prayer

Loving God, thank you for the gift of this day and the opportunity to grow in relationship with you. As we pick up our cross to follow you, we know that we do not do so alone, for you are ever with us. Keep us keenly aware of your presence, that we might remain faithful to your Gospel and the way of life to which we are called. **Amen**.

In today's gospel we hear the parable of the Prodigal Son, perhaps better called the parable of the Merciful Father. Knowing that God is abundant in mercy, we call to mind our own sins and ask for God's forgiveness and healing . . .

Prayer

Patient God,
you wait for us, unwearyingly, to return to you
and to again live in your love.
When we stray and are lost, place this prayer on our lips:
"[We] will rise and go to [our] father."
You will welcome us with loving arms and eternal mercy.
Amen.

Gospel   Luke 15:1-32 (or Luke 15:1-10)

Tax collectors and sinners were all drawing near to listen to Jesus, but the Pharisees and scribes began to complain, saying, "This man welcomes sinners and eats with them." So to them he addressed this parable. "What man among you having a hundred sheep and losing one of them would not leave the ninety-nine in the desert and go after the lost one until he finds it? And when he does find it, he sets it on his shoulders with great joy and, upon his arrival home, he calls together his friends and neighbors and says to them, 'Rejoice with me because I have found my lost sheep.' I tell you, in just the same way there will be more joy in heaven over one sinner who repents than over ninety-nine righteous people who have no need of repentance.

"Or what woman having ten coins and losing one would not light a lamp and sweep the house, searching carefully until she finds it? And when she does find it, she calls together her friends and neighbors and says to them, 'Rejoice with me because I have found the coin that I lost.' In just the same way, I tell you, there will be rejoicing among the angels of God over one sinner who repents."

Then he said, "A man had two sons, and the younger son said to his father, 'Father give me the share of your estate that should come to me.' So the father divided the property between them. After a few days, the younger son collected all his belongings and set off to a distant country where he squandered his inheritance on a life of dissipation. When he had freely spent everything, a severe famine struck that country, and he found himself in dire need. So he hired himself out to one of the local citizens who sent him to his farm to tend the swine. And he longed to eat his fill of the pods on which the swine fed, but nobody gave him any. Coming to his senses he thought, 'How many of my father's hired workers have more than enough food to eat, but here am I, dying from hunger. I shall get up and go to my father and I shall say to him, "Father, I have sinned against heaven and against you. I no longer deserve to be called your son; treat me as you would treat one of your hired workers."' So he got up and went back to his father. While he was still a long way off, his father caught sight of him, and was filled with compassion. He ran to his son, embraced him and kissed him. His son said to him, 'Father, I have sinned against heaven and against you; I no longer deserve to be called your son.' But his father ordered his servants, 'Quickly bring the finest robe and put it on him; put a ring on his finger and sandals on his feet. Take the fattened calf and slaughter it. Then let us celebrate with a feast, because this son of mine was dead, and has come to life again; he was lost, and has been found.' Then the celebration began. Now the older son had been out in the field and, on his way back, as he neared the house, he heard the sound of music and dancing. He called one of the servants and asked what this might mean. The servant said to him, 'Your brother has returned and your father has slaughtered the fattened calf because he has him back safe and sound.' He became angry, and when he refused to enter the house, his father came out and pleaded with him. He said to his father in reply, 'Look, all these years I served you and not once did I disobey your orders; yet you never gave me even a young goat to feast on with my friends. But when your son returns, who swallowed up your property with prostitutes, for him you slaughter the fattened calf.' He said to him, 'My son, you are here with me always; everything I have is yours. But now we must celebrate and rejoice, because your brother was dead and has come to life again; he was lost and has been found.'"

Brief Silence

For Reflection

The parable of the Prodigal Son can be regarded as the gospel in miniature, announcing as it does the compassionate love of God that forgives and welcomes home the sinner. In giving his sons their inheritance, the father makes his first gesture of radical, "foolish" love, allowing the younger boy the freedom to leave home. The son had no intention of ending up in a pigsty, but that is where he eventually finds himself—starving and impoverished, both materially and spiritually.

When he goes out to welcome his son back home, the father again shows his foolish, costly love. There is no cool, reserved reception of his son, but a running welcome, a kiss, a compassionate embrace that squeezes all the preconceived plans out of his son. All the boy can say is: "Father, I have sinned against heaven and against you; I no longer deserve to be called your son." And from their dead relationships, his father raises him to new life, newly clothed and feasted.

The parable of the Prodigal Son shows us an image of our Father who is also prodigal—a spendthrift with his love for each one of us, his unadorned and vulnerable children.

✦ Which character in today's gospel do you most identify with? Why?

Brief Silence

Prayer

Loving God, thank you for the gift of this day and the opportunity to grow in relationship with you. We turn away all too often, yet you remain steadfast in your love and mercy, calling us back to you. Keep us mindful of our need for reconciliation and relationship, that we might remain faithful to your Gospel and the way of life to which we are called. **Amen**.

In today's gospel Jesus reminds us we cannot serve two masters. For the times we have placed other people or things in front of God, we ask for forgiveness . . .

Prayer

God of the Margins,
you are enthroned in the heavens,
yet lift the lowly from the dust.
You, *who lifts up the poor,* are God of us all.
Raise us, make us aware of the dignity you have bestowed on us.
Our worth is only found in you.
Amen.

Gospel   Luke 16:1-13 (or Luke 16:10-13)

Jesus said to his disciples, "A rich man had a steward who was reported to him for squandering his property. He summoned him and said, 'What is this I hear about you? Prepare a full account of your stewardship, because you can no longer be my steward.' The steward said to himself, 'What shall I do, now that my master is taking the position of steward away from me? I am not strong enough to dig and I am ashamed to beg. I know what I shall do so that, when I am removed from the stewardship, they may welcome me into their homes.' He called in his master's debtors one by one. To the first he said, 'How much do you owe my master?' He replied, 'One hundred measures of olive oil.' He said to him, 'Here is your promissory note. Sit down and quickly write one for fifty.' Then to another the steward said, 'And you, how much do you owe?'

He replied, 'One hundred kors of wheat.' The steward said to him, 'Here is your promissory note; write one for eighty.' And the master commended that dishonest steward for acting prudently.

"For the children of this world are more prudent in dealing with their own generation than are the children of light. I tell you, make friends for yourselves with dishonest wealth, so that when it fails, you will be welcomed into eternal dwellings. The person who is trustworthy in very small matters is also trustworthy in great ones; and the person who is dishonest in very small matters is also dishonest in great ones. If, therefore, you are not trustworthy with dishonest wealth, who will trust you with true wealth? If you are not trustworthy with what belongs to another, who will give you what is yours? No servant can serve two masters. He will either hate one and love the other, or be devoted to one and despise the other. You cannot serve both God and mammon."

Brief Silence

For Reflection

Probably none of us will ever feature in the list of the world's top billionaires but, says Jesus, it is the one who can be trusted with little things who can be trusted with the great and so win a rich inheritance in the kingdom. It is easy to be irresponsible with the familiar, everyday tasks, harboring the illusion that we will be reliable and committed when the big demands come. But most of us in the near future will not have a stunning success on the stock market, launch a scheme for global economic recovery, or die a martyr's death. More likely, we will contribute to or disregard our parish planned giving; buy or resist purchasing what we don't really need; recycle our garbage or destroy a few more trees. The mundane is rich in opportunities for storing up treasure in heaven. If we are tainted with acquisitiveness, the best thing to do with our money is to give it away to those in need. Although we may not be introduced to them until we meet in the kingdom, our generous initiative will win us friends among the poor who are raised up, the hungry who are filled.

✦ Does it ever feel like you are trying to serve two masters, either intentionally or unintentionally? If so, how might you refocus your attention to God?

Brief Silence

Prayer

Loving God, thank you for the gift of this day and the opportunity to grow in relationship with you. Sometimes we try to serve two masters, yet you are not vengeful. Call us back to you that we might stand firm in our faith so to remain faithful to your Gospel and the way of life to which we are called. **Amen**.

There are times in our lives that we fall short of living who we are called to be. Knowing this, we ask for God's forgiveness and healing . . .

Prayer

God of Authentic Freedom,
you give justice to the oppressed,
food to the hungry, and raise all those
    bent low.
Help us to see in ourselves the Beatitudes,
and to know in you true freedom and joy.
Praise the Lord!
Amen.

Gospel   Luke 16:19-31

Jesus said to the Pharisees: "There was a rich man who dressed in purple garments and fine linen and dined sumptuously each day. And lying at his door was a poor man named Lazarus, covered with sores, who would gladly have eaten his fill of the scraps that fell from the rich man's table. Dogs even used to come and lick his sores. When the poor man died, he was carried away by angels to the bosom of Abraham. The rich man also died and was buried, and from the netherworld, where he was in torment, he raised his eyes and saw Abraham far off and Lazarus at his side. And he cried out, 'Father Abraham, have pity on me. Send Lazarus to dip the tip of his finger in water and cool my tongue for I am suffering torment in these flames.' Abraham replied, 'My child, remember that you received what was good during your lifetime while Lazarus likewise received what was bad; but now he is comforted here, whereas you are tormented. Moreover, between us and you a great chasm is established to prevent anyone from crossing who might wish to go from our side to yours or from your side to ours.' He said, 'Then I beg you, father, send him to my father's house, for I have five brothers, so that he may warn them, lest they too come to this place of torment.' But Abraham replied, 'They have

Moses and the prophets. Let them listen to them.' He said, 'Oh no, father Abraham, but if someone from the dead goes to them, they will repent.' Then Abraham said, 'If they will not listen to Moses and the prophets, neither will they be persuaded if someone should rise from the dead.'"

Brief Silence

For Reflection

We listen to the parable of the Rich Man and Lazarus, gathered together by the one who has risen from the dead and comes to us in his Word and sacrament. Is our liturgical celebration securely and comfortably "gated" from the "poor" outside? Or does it challenge us to welcome and serve them? Do we ever allow ourselves to be challenged by those who are covered with the contemporary "sores" of unemployment, disabilities, need for asylum, abuse? When "the poor" are just an abstract concept, they continue to be separated from us by a great chasm.

We must try to bridge the chasm in whatever way we can: through personal generosity, individual and group advocacy, information that stirs the heart to outreach, ethical business investments, or responsible voting; we are called to respond to the word of God in *this* life. Like the rich man and his five brothers, no signs, no miracles, not even the word of God, can break into and convert our hearts if we are determined to lock out the disadvantaged from our lives, because in them our poor brother Jesus still sits begging at our gates.

✦ What image or images of God does today's gospel bring to mind for you?

Brief Silence

Prayer

Loving God, thank you for the gift of this day and the opportunity to grow in relationship with you. We know what you ask of us: to love you and others without exception. Nudge us often to look beyond our own selves that we might remain faithful to your Gospel and the way of life to which we are called. **Amen**.

In today's gospel the disciples ask Jesus to increase their faith. For the times we have not been faithful to God's call in our lives, we ask for forgiveness and healing . . .

Prayer

God, Rock and Foundation,
if today we hear your voice,
if today we bow in worship,
if today we kneel before you,
do not turn away from us, but let us cling to you,
and acclaim you our maker and our salvation,
you who reign for ever and ever.
Amen.

Gospel
Luke 17:5-10

The apostles said to the Lord, "Increase our faith." The Lord replied, "If you have faith the size of a mustard seed, you would say to this mulberry tree, 'Be uprooted and planted in the sea,' and it would obey you.

"Who among you would say to your servant who has just come in from plowing or tending sheep in the field, 'Come here immediately and take your place at table'? Would he not rather say to him, 'Prepare something for me to eat. Put on your apron and wait on me while I eat and drink. You may eat and drink when I am finished'? Is he grateful to that servant because he did what was commanded? So should it be with you. When you have done all you have been commanded, say, 'We are unprofitable servants; we have done what we were obliged to do.'"

Brief Silence

For Reflection

This gospel comes immediately after some hard words of Jesus to his disciples: warnings about being a stumbling block for others on the journey of discipleship. What is needed is correction, repentance, and forgiveness that is generous and uncalculating, even in aggravating circumstances. It all seems a bit too much for the disciples, so they cry, in the verse that opens our reading, "Increase our faith."

"Quality, not quantity" is a cliché that we often use, seriously or frivolously, with reference to many different situations. In this one, the apostles (not the larger group of disciples) are asking Jesus for "more" faith, but Jesus responds with a qualitative image of faith: faith that is like a tiny mustard seed which the Sower God plants in our hearts. Buried deep, it germinates in darkness, but if we fail to tend the seed it will never break through its protective membrane and push into our lives. When disciples do live by faith, even "mustard seed faith," they can continue to do extraordinary things like persisting in the forgiveness about which Jesus has just spoken in the verse preceding the Lectionary text.

✦ How would you describe your faith? Have you ever prayed to increase your faith?

Brief Silence

Prayer

Loving God, thank you for the gift of this day and the opportunity to grow in relationship with you. When we try to quantify grace, love, or faith, we quickly realize that our relationship with you is not about numbers or quotas. Open our hearts for relationship so that we might know you more deeply as we strive to remain faithful to your Gospel and the way of life to which we are called. **Amen**.

In today's gospel ten lepers call out to Jesus, "Have pity on us!" Knowing there are places in our own lives in need of healing, we ask for God's forgiveness and peace . . .

Prayer

Wondrous God,
your victories for us make known your salvation,
for you *revealed to the nations* your *saving power.*
Instill in us your faithfulness, that we too may be faithful;
show us your kindness, that we too may be kind.
Amen.

Gospel   Luke 17:11-19

As Jesus continued his journey to Jerusalem, he traveled through Samaria and Galilee. As he was entering a village, ten lepers met him. They stood at a distance from him and raised their voices, saying, "Jesus, Master! Have pity on us!" And when he saw them, he said, "Go show yourselves to the priests." As they were going they were cleansed. And one of them, realizing he had been healed, returned, glorifying God in a loud voice; and he fell at the feet of Jesus and thanked him. He was a Samaritan. Jesus said in reply, "Ten were cleansed, were they not? Where are the other nine? Has none but this foreigner returned to give thanks to God?" Then he said to him, "Stand up and go; your faith has saved you."

Brief Silence

For Reflection

The significance of "seeing" is repeated throughout today's gospel. Jesus sees those who need mercy; the lepers see they are healed; and one of them sees the power and presence of God in his healing. Disciples need to learn how to "see" and be moved with compassion. Thomas Merton described being overwhelmed on a street corner in Louisville: "I found that everything stirred me with a deep and mute sense of compassion. Perhaps some of the people we saw going about the streets were hard and tough—but I did not observe it because I seemed to have lost an eye for merely exterior detail and to have discovered, instead, a deep sense of respect and love" (*The Sign of Jonas*).

Do we see today's "lepers" in the isolated, the alienated, the "untouchables" in our society, and respond with compassion? And what of the "leper" in each one of us: that weakest, least acceptable, and most unattractive aspect of myself that seems to distance me from God, from my sisters and brothers, and from my own self-acceptance? For all this, we, too, need to cry out with faith, "Jesus, Master! Have pity on us!"

✦ How do you practice gratitude?

Brief Silence

Prayer

Loving God, thank you for the gift of this day and the opportunity to grow in relationship with you. Saying "thank you" should be so easy, yet practicing gratitude does not always come naturally. Open our eyes and our hearts to your works so that we have no choice but to abound in gratitude as we strive to remain faithful to your Gospel and the way of life to which we are called. **Amen**.

In today's gospel Jesus reminds his disciples of the importance of praying without becoming weary. For the times we have grown weary in prayer or discipleship, we ask for God's healing and peace . . .

Prayer

Lord who Made Heaven and Earth,
you are our help and neither slumber nor sleep.
Watch over us always, guardian and shield,
be with us on every journey, to you and with you,
one in holiness and love.
Amen.

Gospel   Luke 18:1-8

Jesus told his disciples a parable about the necessity for them to pray always without becoming weary. He said, "There was a judge in a certain town who neither feared God nor respected any human being. And a widow in that town used to come to him and say, 'Render a just decision for me against my adversary.' For a long time the judge was unwilling, but eventually he thought, 'While it is true that I neither fear God nor respect any human being, because this widow keeps bothering me I shall deliver a just decision for her lest she finally come and strike me.'" The Lord said, "Pay attention to what the dishonest judge says. Will not God then secure the rights of his chosen ones who call out to him day and night? Will he be slow to answer them? I tell you, he will see to it that justice is done for them speedily. But when the Son of Man comes, will he find faith on earth?"

Brief Silence

For Reflection

The judge in today's parable is described as dishonest and contemptuous in order to put him in sharp contrast with God. If even a judge like this one gave in to the widow because of self-interest and suspect motives, how much more, suggests Jesus, will our compassionate God do justice for those who persist in their prayer and their faith. The destitute and the despised, those with no voting power, those on the losing side, are offered in the person of Jesus the presence and grace of God. Jesus's disciples, therefore, are to persist in prayer and be accountable for justice, advocating for people on the margins and enabling the defenseless to find their own voices, because what is not just is not of God.

To prayer that is persistent and constant must also be added the qualities of trust and patience that support the belief that God answers persevering prayer when and how God wills. The timeline may be lengthy, and faith must endure until the coming of the Son of Man at the end of our own personal life and also until the Second Coming at the end of human history.

✦ How do you practice perseverance in faith?

Brief Silence

Prayer

Loving God, thank you for the gift of this day and the opportunity to grow in relationship with you. We know you hear us when we pray, and you never tire of listening. May we never tire of reaching out to you as we strive to remain faithful to your Gospel and the way of life to which we are called. **Amen**.

In today's gospel Jesus invites us to humble ourselves so that we might be exalted. For the times we have not practiced humility, we ask for God's forgiveness . . .

Prayer

Lord of the Brokenhearted,
your ears are attentive to all who call to you,
for you hear *the cry of the poor.*
You stand against those who bring forth evil,
and raise those weighed down by sin and death.
We praise your holy name!
Amen.

Gospel   Luke 18:9-14

Jesus addressed this parable to those who were convinced of their own righteousness and despised everyone else. "Two people went up to the temple area to pray; one was a Pharisee and the other was a tax collector. The Pharisee took up his position and spoke this prayer to himself, 'O God, I thank you that I am not like the rest of humanity—greedy, dishonest, adulterous—or even like this tax collector. I fast twice a week, and I pay tithes on my whole income.' But the tax collector stood off at a distance and would not even raise his eyes to heaven but beat his breast and prayed, 'O God, be merciful to me a sinner.' I tell you, the latter went home justified, not the former; for whoever exalts himself will be humbled, and the one who humbles himself will be exalted."

Brief Silence

For Reflection

From the beginning to the end of this parable, Jesus draws a sharp contrast between the two men who go to the temple to pray. The Pharisee stood and prayed about himself in a litany of self-congratulation: "I . . . , I . . . , I . . . ." Exalted in his own eyes, the Pharisee looks down on others, adding the tax collector to his list of undesirable companions or worshippers. He announces it not only to God (in case God doesn't know) but also to the other worshipers around him. If we are regular churchgoers and financial supporters of our parish, it might be shocking but sobering to stand with the Pharisee, rather than the tax collector, and look into our own hearts. How dependent on God do see ourselves to be? How self-satisfied are we about our religious observance? Are we dismissive of or mean-spirited about those who are on the margins of church and society, or outside both? And how do such attitudes and judgments affect our relationship with God and our prayer life? The love of God can so easily turn into idolatrous self-love.

✦ How is God inviting you to grow in humility today?

Brief Silence

Prayer

Loving God, thank you for the gift of this day and the opportunity to grow in relationship with you. Give us the self-awareness to know both our strengths and our weakness, and give us the courage to bring all to you in prayer so to remain faithful to your Gospel and the way of life to which we are called. **Amen**.

In today's gospel Zacchaeus turns to Jesus and acknowledges his sins. Let us do the same, asking for God's pardon and peace . . .

Prayer

God who Reigns,
your graciousness and mercy are without end;
you are good and kind to all.
[We] will praise your name forever,
and tell all with ears of your faithfulness and truth.
Every day is filled with your love.
Amen.

Gospel   Luke 19:1-10

At that time, Jesus came to Jericho and intended to pass through the town. Now a man there named Zacchaeus, who was a chief tax collector and also a wealthy man, was seeking to see who Jesus was; but he could not see him because of the crowd, for he was short in stature. So he ran ahead and climbed a sycamore tree in order to see Jesus, who was about to pass that way. When he reached the place, Jesus looked up and said, "Zacchaeus, come down quickly, for today I must stay at your house." And he came down quickly and received him with joy. When they all saw this, they began to grumble, saying, "He has gone to stay at the house of a sinner." But Zacchaeus stood there and said to the Lord, "Behold, half of my possessions, Lord, I shall give to the poor, and if I have extorted anything from anyone I shall repay it four times over." And Jesus said to him, "Today salvation has come to this house because this man too is a descendant of Abraham. For the Son of Man has come to seek and to save what was lost."

Brief Silence

For Reflection

Jesus invites himself to Zacchaeus's house; he is host rather than guest, offering the tax collector the hospitality of salvation. Jesus longs to be welcomed into our homes, our parishes, our communities, and be received there with joy—the expansive Lukan response to the good news. Then, to our surprise, we too will find ourselves hosted into new life and love.

The murmuring crowd is nameless, and we can ask ourselves if we are in its midst: rejecting others because of prejudice and cynical superiority that "knows" what certain people are like and that they cannot change. Yet Jesus keeps company with "the lost," and the vividness of the account gives Zacchaeus a very human face. Although a meal at Zacchaeus's house is not part of the narrative, it is only a threshold away. Because Jesus so often encounters despised people and offers them hospitality, questions are surely raised for the church: "Who should we welcome into the reign of God?" and "With whom should we eat?" The answer to the first is universal; the answer to the second is an ongoing quest that dares to question.

✦ Just as Zacchaeus climbed the tree to see Jesus, what do you do to make yourself available to God?

Brief Silence

Prayer

Loving God, thank you for the gift of this day and the opportunity to grow in relationship with you. Clear our hearts and minds of the distractions that keep us from you, and empower us to stand before you without reservation as we remain faithful to your Gospel and the way of life to which we are called. **Amen.**

Today's celebration of All Saints reminds us that you call each of us to holiness. May this water remind us of our own baptismal vocation . . .

Prayer

Lord,
you who made all things,
this is the people that longs to see
your face.
You are mystery among us, show us your presence;
you are blessing and holiness, show us your life.
Be with us always, and help us to know you more fully.
Amen.

Gospel   Matt 5:1-12a

When Jesus saw the crowds, he went up the mountain, and after he had sat down, his disciples came to him. He began to teach them, saying: / "Blessed are the poor in spirit, / for theirs is the Kingdom of heaven. / Blessed are they who mourn, / for they will be comforted. / Blessed are the meek, / for they will inherit the land. / Blessed are they who hunger and thirst for righteousness, / for they will be satisfied. / Blessed are the merciful, / for they will be shown mercy. / Blessed are the clean of heart, / for they will see God. / Blessed are the peacemakers, / for they will be called children of God. / Blessed are they who are persecuted for the sake of righteousness, / for theirs is the Kingdom of heaven. / Blessed are you when they insult you and persecute you and utter every kind of evil against you falsely because of me. Rejoice and be glad, for your reward will be great in heaven."

Brief Silence

For Reflection

The saints are servants of God because they shared in God's plan for the salvation of the world and their presence to everyone was a testament of their "children of God" identity (1 John 3:1) who were obedient only to the will and plan of God. As the children of God, Jesus's Sermon on the Mount was a way of life for the saints (Matt 5:1-12). The saints aspired to deal justly in their actions, doing what was right and upright before God and humankind. As the children of God who had committed themselves to the teachings of Jesus and the Christian life, they have been rewarded with eternal life.

Today, we honor them for their forbearing life of holiness and faith in Christ. They were simply living the values of their familial relationship with God on account of their baptism in Christ. Like us, they were members of a family, community, and nation. Therefore, we are capable of the life of holiness and Christian charity like the saints. In effect, we too will join the communion of saints in the company of angels and in perpetual adoration of God (Rev 7:9-12).

✦ We are all called to be saints. How do you feel about this reality?

Brief Silence

Prayer

Loving God, thank you for the gift of this day and the opportunity to grow in relationship with you. You give us examples of holy women and men of faith who showed by their lives how we should live. May we call on their intercession without hesitation, and look to them often as we remain faithful to your Gospel and the way of life to which we are called. **Amen**.

As we commemorate those who have died, we recognize and name the times in our lives where we have failed to respond to God's invitation to love and ask for healing and forgiveness . . .

Prayer

Lord, [Our] Shepherd,
in the darkness, we know no fear,
when afraid, we know courage and safety.
You give this and more to us,
there is nothing [we] shall want.
Abide with us all our days,
and let us dwell in your house forever.
Amen.

Gospel   **John 6:37-40***

Jesus said to the crowds: "Everything that the Father gives me will come to me, and I will not reject anyone who comes to me, because I came down from heaven not to do my own will but the will of the one who sent me. And this is the will of the one who sent me, that I should not lose anything of what he gave me, but that I should raise it on the last day. For this is the will of my Father, that everyone who sees the Son and believes in him may have eternal life, and I shall raise him up on the last day."

Brief Silence

For Reflection

We celebrate the feast of All Souls with the firm belief that they have joined the company of the holy ones in the presence of God. They identified with Christ's life, death, and resurrection because baptism had made them one with Christ: "For all of you who were baptized into Christ have clothed yourselves with Christ" (Gal 3:27). The benefits of their baptism in Christ reached its fullness in their experience of resurrection from the dead and newness of life (Rom 6:4). This is because to conform one's life according to the Christian rite of baptism leads to the experience of the eternal life that Christ promises.

Those who are initiated through baptism in the "name of Christ Jesus" lived the life of Christ whose identity they have embraced. For this reason, they will experience the resurrection from the dead just as Christ had experienced (Rom 6:5). On this feast of All Souls, we honor those who died in Christ asking for their prayer for us. Also, let us turn our memorial for the faithful departed into an occasion for us to renew our commitment to God through Christ.

✦ What are your experiences of death and loss? What role did/does your faith play in these experiences?

Brief Silence

Prayer

Loving God, thank you for the gift of this day and the opportunity to grow in relationship with you. We have been baptized into your life, death, and resurrection. May this reality bring us the hope we need to follow you without reservation as we remain faithful to your Gospel and the way of life to which we are called. **Amen**.

*Other gospel options for November 2:

Matthew 5:1-12a / Matthew 11:25-30 / Matthew 25:31-46 / Luke 7:11-17 / Luke 23:44-46, 50, 52-53; 24:1-6a / Luke 24:13-16, 28-35 / John 5:24-29 / John 6:51-58 / John 11:17-27 / John 11:32-45 / John 14:1-6

Today the psalmist proclaims, "My steps have been steadfast in your paths, my feet have not faltered." For the times we have not been steadfast and turned away from God, we ask for forgiveness, healing, and peace . . .

Prayer
Lord,
you hear the words of the meek and lowly,
and raise all to dignity beyond all measure.
When your glory appears, [our] joy will be full,
and our cup will overflow with your love and justice.
Let it cover the earth, that all may know you and your splendor.
Amen.

Gospel   **Luke 20:27, 34-38 (or Luke 20:27-38)**

Some Sadducees, those who deny that there is a resurrection, came forward.

Jesus said to them, "The children of this age marry and re-marry; but those who are deemed worthy to attain to the coming age and to the resurrection of the dead neither marry nor are given in marriage. They can no longer die, for they are like angels; and they are the children of God because they are the ones who will rise. That the dead will rise even Moses made known in the passage about the bush, when he called out 'Lord,' the God of Abraham, the God of Isaac, and the God of Jacob; and he is not God of the dead, but of the living, for to him all are alive."

Brief Silence

For Reflection

In today's gospel, Jesus refuses to play number games or trivial biblical pursuit with the Sadducees. The power of resurrection is utterly new and overwhelmingly transformative. To be children of the resurrection is to be ready to commit ourselves into the hands of God, accepting that our relationship with God surpasses any other human relationship, no matter how intimate and loving. Jesus shows the Sadducees that they are playing with fire when they try to use the Word of God against him. He replies in a traditional Jewish method, answering their reference to one biblical text with another, and giving it a meaning that extends beyond that of the original author. Unlike the Sadducees' biblical reference, the text that Jesus quotes is radical and central to Jewish faith: the event of the burning bush (Exod 3). Here, says Jesus, God names himself as the "I AM," the God of Abraham, Isaac, and Jacob, a God in a continuing and personal relationship with the Hebrew ancestors that transcends death. This is "not God of the dead, but of the living, / for to him all are alive." This is the fierce faith that is the central focus and challenge of the gospel.

✦ What does belief in the resurrection mean to you?

Brief Silence

Prayer

Loving God, thank you for the gift of this day and the opportunity to grow in relationship with you. You raise each of us to life in you and show us the incredible power of self-gift. May we freely give of ourselves for others, so to remain faithful to your Gospel and the way of life to which we are called. **Amen**.

As we come to the end of the liturgical year, we take a moment to reflect on the ways we have failed to be the people God calls us to be and ask for God's forgiveness . . .

Prayer

Almighty God,
you are maker of mountains and master
    of seas;
you come *to rule the earth with justice.*
Let all creation cry to you, in praise
    and joy,
for your justice and equity bring all to perfect holiness,
and unity in you.
Amen.

Gospel   Luke 21:5-19

While some people were speaking about how the temple was adorned with costly stones and votive offerings, Jesus said, "All that you see here—the days will come when there will not be left a stone upon another stone that will not be thrown down."

Then they asked him, "Teacher, when will this happen? And what sign will there be when all these things are about to happen?" He answered, "See that you not be deceived, for many will come in my name, saying, 'I am he,' and 'The time has come.' Do not follow them! When you hear of wars and insurrections, do not be terrified; for such things must happen first, but it will not immediately be the end." Then he said to them, "Nation will rise against nation, and kingdom against kingdom. There will be powerful earthquakes, famines, and plagues from place to place; and awesome sights and mighty signs will come from the sky.

"Before all this happens, however, they will seize and persecute you, they will hand you over to the synagogues and to prisons, and they will have you led before kings and governors because of my name. It will lead to your giving testimony. Remember, you are not to prepare your defense beforehand, for I myself shall give you a wisdom in speaking that all your adversaries will be powerless to resist or refute. You will even be handed over by parents, brothers, relatives, and friends, and they will put some of you to death. You will be hated by all because of my name, but not a hair on your head will be destroyed. By your perseverance you will secure your lives."

Brief Silence

For Reflection

Jesus warns us today to watch out for—but not be deceived by or panicked because of—prophets of doom. There will be persecutions and suffering, betrayals even by family and friends, but these are opportunities to bear witness to one's faith. There is no need to worry about what to say. The Lord will never allow his faithful witness to perish.

Jesus is not forecasting the end *of* the world; he is urging his followers to confidence in and obedience to God in the face of the tough demands of their present and future discipleship that is *for* the world. In the Acts of the Apostles, Luke describes how the early church suffered the various trials Jesus speaks about in this gospel: imprisonment, persecution, hatred. But this was countered by the bold wisdom of Stephen, the apostles' empowerment to work miracles on hearts and bodies, their steadfastness in prison or under flogging and, ultimately, martyrdom. This is what Jesus himself suffered, and with Jesus we can let go of our precious, protected selves, confident that, no matter what the disaster, if we die into his love, we will also rise with him.

✦ How have you come to know that God is God not of the dead, but of the living?

Brief Silence

Prayer

Loving God, thank you for the gift of this day and the opportunity to grow in relationship with you. You call us your precious children, beloved and chosen by you. Help us to truly live as your beloved, knowing our worth and value, so we may remain faithful to your Gospel and the way of life to which we are called. **Amen**.

In today's gospel the repentant thief calls out to Jesus on the cross and asks for mercy. We, too, ask for God's forgiveness for the times we have failed to love as we should . . .

Prayer

God of All,
you prepare for each of us a dwelling
        place,
where all are welcome, and all know joy.
Let us go rejoicing to the house of the Lord.
Bring us to you, one in love, joy, and strength,
you who live and reign for ever and ever.
Amen.

Gospel   **Luke 23:35-43**

The rulers sneered at Jesus and said, "He saved others, let him save himself if he is the chosen one, the Christ of God." Even the soldiers jeered at him. As they approached to offer him wine they called out, "If you are King of the Jews, save yourself." Above him there was an inscription that read, "This is the King of the Jews."

Now one of the criminals hanging there reviled Jesus, saying, "Are you not the Christ? Save yourself and us." The other, however, rebuking him, said in reply, "Have you no fear of God, for you are subject to the same condemnation? And indeed, we have been condemned justly, for the sentence we received corresponds to our crimes, but this man has done nothing criminal." Then he said,

"Jesus, remember me when you come into your kingdom." He replied to him, "Amen, I say to you, today you will be with me in Paradise."

Brief Silence

For Reflection

Around Jesus as he hangs on his cross in the gospel for this solemnity of Christ the King are people who will rise because of him: those who stand by not just watching but "contemplating" their crucified king and the criminal who recognizes in Jesus an authority so different from that which has condemned them both. Luke gives to this man the voice of a traditional Jewish hope for the end time that was envisaged as a return to the primeval innocence and peace of the garden ("Paradise"). Throughout his life, Jesus had associated with and befriended outcasts, sought out and forgave the lost and the sinners; he will do this even as he is dying. One of the crucified criminals rebukes the other for his cynical messianic taunting of Jesus and dares to ask Jesus for a late invitation into the kingdom. This criminal addresses him not with the title of the inscription hanging above him, but simply and familiarly as "Jesus." And then a faint, future hope becomes a "today" event of salvation for him, the man for whom the compassion of Jesus throws open the door of the kingdom and allows him to steal Paradise.

✦ What does it mean to say God's kingdom is both "here" and "not yet"?

Brief Silence

Prayer

Loving God, thank you for the gift of this day and the opportunity to grow in relationship with you. You are a king who reigns with love, not terror, peace, not violence, and generosity, not selfishness. May we work to bring about the reality of your kingdom here on earth, so to remain faithful to your Gospel and the way of life to which we are called. **Amen**.